A Hunt For Life's Extras

THE STORY OF

ARCHIBALD RUTLEDGE

For my friend, Kim
who shares my admiration
for Archibald Rutledge

Paula Bode

OTHER BOOKS BY IDELLA BODIE

The Secret of Telfair Inn
Ghost in the Capitol
The Mystery of the Pirate's Treasure
Stranded!
South Carolina Women: They Dared to Lead

Idella
Bodie

A Hunt For Lifes Extras

THE STORY OF

ARCHIBALD

RUTLEDGE

Authors Choice Press
San Jose New York Lincoln Shanghai

A Hunt For Life's Extras
The Story of Archibald Rutledge

Authors Choice Press
an imprint of iUniverse.com, Inc.

For information address:
iUniverse.com, Inc.
5220 S 16th, Ste. 200
Lincoln, NE 68512
www.iuniverse.com

Originally published by Sandlapper

ISBN: 0-595-15113-2

Printed in the United States of America

For Rose Wilkins,
who saw the need for such
a work
for the youth of South
Carolina

Archibald Rutledge

Prologue

At the turn of the century Archibald Rutledge, South Carolina's poet laureate for thirty-nine years, was growing up in the coastal region of Carolina.

Born into one of South Carolina's most distinguished families, Archibald Rutledge grew up in an era that has passed. Yet he has preserved human experiences that continue to influence persons of all ages and all times. His deep reverence for God's world is reflected in his poetry and prose.

It gives me a special joy to share with young readers the beauty and mystery of life as seen through the eyes of this sensitive poet, teacher, hunter, and philosopher.

I wish to thank R.L. Bryan and Fleming H. Revell Company for permission to use copyrighted material and pictures.

My sincere appreciation to Mrs. Loulie Latimer Owens for her preparation of the papers of Archibald Hamilton Rutledge; to Mr. Kenneth Toombs, Director of Libraries of the University of South Carolina; to Mr. E.L. Inabinet and the staff of the Manuscript Depart-

ment of South Caroliniana Library; to the Honorable
Irvine H. Rutledge, youngest son of Archibald
Rutledge; and to Rose Wilkins for requesting a
biography of South Carolina's first poet laureate for the
youth of South Carolina.

One

Archie sank to his lean ankles in the sedge and brackish water of the vast Santee delta. Prince, his inseparable young Negro companion hurried to keep up. Each step away from Hampton Plantation and across the spongy sawgrass made them more aware of the blind ditches and the treacherous bog of Bellefield rice land.

Already vultures swooped and circled over the marsh wasteland. Were they too late?

Earlier the boys had stood watching the evening feeding and milking at the stable lot.

"Boss man," Prince's father had said to Archie's father, Colonel Rutledge, "that little old Ruby, she didn't come up last night. And that calf been bawling all day. I'se 'fraid she done bogged down."

Hearing that, Archie and Prince struck out for the wild overgrown rice field along the Santee River. With growths of wampee, sawgrass, and duck oats brushing their legs, they hurried toward the fearful quicksand.

In early spring the woods furnished little food for hungry cattle, and the vivid green of the waste field beckoned them, only to bog them in mire.

And because of the cleft in the cows' hoofs their struggles only sank their weakened bodies deeper in the muddy bog.

Now that Bellefield rice land was no longer planted, no one went to the remote and lonely fields for weeks at a time. As a result, mired animals often starved before help came. Worse still, vultures pecked the dark velvet eyes from their heads. With a shudder Archie remembered the old plow ox, Mose.

And now Ruby was there. If she wasn't, she would have come home last night. Nothing else could have kept her from her newly born calf. If only Will hadn't turned her out to forage, but then feed for cattle was scarce on the plantation in March. Or, if he had only told them earlier that Ruby was missing.

Archie remembered just three weeks ago when he and Prince had found the little red cow and her newborn baby in a pine thicket. The proud mother with her spindly red-and-white calf lay on a sunny bed of broomsedge. Ruby was standing watch, the pride of motherhood in her eyes.

The two boys struggled over the rail fence that Colonel Rutledge had put up between Hampton Plantation and Bellefield. Even that had not kept the cows from the tempting green grass growing on the other side. They would swim around the fence where it came to an end in the river and wade ashore on the fated Bellefield tract.

For some reason the animals who survived the bog never had enough sense to swim back around the fence. Archie had seen workers take down the fence to admit lowing cattle to the other side and safety.

The sun cast a ruddy glow behind Archie and Prince as they made their way toward the deceptive field. Of the two places the young boys held in mortal terror, one was the Negro burial ground and the other the quicksand of Bellefield rice land.

Ahead, mist from the river was beginning to shroud the tops of craggy black gum and cypress.

"Dere she is!" shouted Prince. "Dere's Ruby. I see her horns gleamin'."

Even from a distance Archie could tell that the little cow was already mired to her back in the mud beneath the grass. Coming nearer, he saw, too, that she had eaten all the grass within reach.

"Poor thing," Archie said, "she probably didn't realize she was sinking until it was too late."

Testing for a solid place to stand, he reached out to stroke the soft hide between her horns. "That's all right, Ruby." he crooned, "we're gonna get you out."

"And jus' how we gonna do that?" Prince threw up his hands in frustration. "'Cause we ain't got no rope."

"Run take down one of the fence rails," Archie directed, "and I'll stay with her so she won't think we're giving her up." He looked above him at the circling buzzards, black against the coming night. Another flock rested atop a dead cypress. No doubt she'd kept them away this long with her sharp horns. At least she could still move her head.

In moments Prince appeared with two rails, and Archie dashed off for two more while Prince caressed Ruby's head.

Working feverishly, they laid two rails parallel to her body and thrust others in the muck beneath her.

When they had secured as solid a footing as they could, Archie gave a signal. They pushed down on the rails with all their strength. Again and again. Then each took hold of a horn and pulled.

Strong little Ruby made every effort to help in the struggle. Once or twice she groaned as if their efforts were useless.

But her sad brown eyes gazing upon them made the boys work all the harder. Little by little and shifting positions and footing, they finally worked her clear. At last she was lifted and pulled and pushed out.

With her mud-caked feet planted on the marsh grass, Ruby trembled from weakness and fright. But at least she was safe.

Archie and Prince had been so busy freeing the little mother they had failed to notice that night was upon them. A chilly mist, rising from the river, was spreading itself in a white veil over the marsh. The woods were a dark outline against the sky, and the stems of grass at their feet had taken on a purplish hue. Except for Ruby's labored breathing, all was silent in dreaded Bellefield.

Stepping carefully, Archie led Ruby by her horns and Prince nudged her from behind. Taking down the rail fence, they trudged once again through the marsh grass leading home. Somewhere behind them a great horned owl sounded his deep creepy call.

Finally they saw a figure with a lantern coming toward them. Archie's father called out.

The happiness the boys felt at arriving safely home with Ruby could not compare with that of the tiny calf to see its mother.

Prince ate supper in the large kitchen of Hampton Plantation, and then as always in their true test of friendship, Archie walked him home. The boys' spirits soared until they reached the Negro burial ground. Here the gloom of the dense thicket surrounding the graves and the great silence that always hovered engulfed them.

At this spot they joined hands and tiptoed by deserted cabins that held spirits of smallpox victims. When they reached the three shadowy pines known as The Three Sisters, they broke away, sending pine needles and sand flying beneath their feet.

The morning after this ritual each boy was always a little surprised that the other had not been carried away by a Plateye, a chimera of the night that carried off children, or a Hiddle-diddle-dee, a great horned owl the Negroes believed was really a spirit masquerading as a bird.

Two

Even though the year was 1900 and Hampton Plantation on the Santee delta of South Carolina had no
modern-day conveniences, Archie never found life dull.

He liked hearing his mother tell of a time when he was
a few months old. She had deposited her little son in his
antique crib in the bedroom and turned to her sewing
when she heard the tell-tale clicking of old Ben's hoofs.

This full-antlered buck had free run of the yard, but
that morning he had come through the front door and
into the bedroom. Archie's mother ran to the room just
as old Ben bowed his great antlers above her baby and
began to nuzzle investigatingly with his cold black nose.

Mrs. Rutledge watched in alarm as Archie crowed
with delight and reached up to catch hold of the brown-
beaded antlers. Just as he was being lifted from his crib
on the massive horns, she yelled and cracked her apron
in the air with a violent flap.

Old Ben took off, bounding through an open window
in a twelve-foot drop to the ground, and left Archie cry-
ing.

Although Archie was too young to remember his close call with old Ben, who later became his friend, he did remember with some misgiving the way he used to taunt the bulls on the plantation. He especially liked to tease Abel, a huge ox with wide-spreading horns, by tickling his heaving nostrils with a broom straw. One day Archie found himself flat on his back with Abel's big eyes staring into his and the great horns pinning him to the ground.

And there was the time he put a poor mud dauber in a real frenzy. This species of small wasp was building his house under a ledge of the plantation porch. He had chosen his spot with great care, for he knew a rain would wash away the wet earth, mostly sand, he was plastering against the wall.

Seeing the dauber at work, Archie sat down with a long cane pole, and each time the little dauber would start his nest, Archie would give it a flick with his cane.

Undaunted, the winged creature would return to the river for another load of mud. But as soon as he had laid his foundation and flown away for more material, Archie would flick it down again. In a few minutes the persistent insect would return with more mud and begin his construction all over again. Although the dauber began to fly around in frustration, he kept making the round trip for more mud.

As Archie watched, he saw to his amazement that the dauber's efforts at construction were changing. The material he was now bringing contained more clay and less sand.

"Why," thought Archie, "he must be thinking that his building material is inferior and is causing his house to fall."

For twenty-one times Archie tore down the dauber's house.

The next day Archie saw that the little dauber had indeed won out. Alongside the nests of many others was one made almost entirely of red clay. He knew without a doubt that this house belonged to the persistent dauber, who now had the strongest house of all.

Even during their son's earliest years, Archie's parents knew that he would be the "different" one of their six children. It was Archie who saw the wild things in the shadows, things his brothers and sisters did not see. It was he who sat for hours studying the intricacies of nature.

Archie's oldest brother, Frederick, had been born of his father's marriage to Anna Maria (Dolly) Blake in 1866. After Dolly's death, Colonel Henry Middleton Rutledge II had married Margaret Hamilton Seabrook, Archibald's mother. This couple had three daughters: Caroline, Harriet, and Mary; and three sons: Thomas, Henry III (Hugh), and Archibald (Archie).

Of Irish and Huguenot ancestry, Archibald had grandfathers on both sides of his family who were governors of South Carolina: John Rutledge and Whitemarsh Seabrook.

When the War Between the States broke out, Archie's father, a tall man with a thin, aquiline nose and blue eyes, lived on an upland farm in Fletcher, North Carolina. Chosen to command the Twenty-fifth North Carolina Regiment, he was cited for bravery at Bull Run and wounded at Malvern Hill and at Sharpsburg. There he was shot from a horse in the Potomac River, but he managed to get to West Virginia, where he rejoined his regiment.

After fighting in Virginia and returning home to a ruined estate and a collapsed civilization, the Colonel, as he was called, continued to wear the gray homespun coat with the patch where a bullet had torn through. Yet

Margaret Hamilton
Seabrook

Col. Henry Middleton
Rutledge II

he never spoke of President Lincoln except kindly. "I tell you," he'd say, "old Abe had a tough job."

Archie's mother to be, who at the time was still Margaret Seabrook, was in constant sympathy with the soldiers. She wrote letters to the front, made clothes for soldiers, wrapped bandages, and prepared medicines.

During this period Margaret, along with other women and children, spent nearly a year as a refugee from the coastal plantations to the piedmont region of the state. Always they were in grave danger of Confederate deserters. When Archie's father returned from the War to the old estate in South Carolina, he married Margaret Seabrook. The year was 1873.

By various means such as renting hunting privileges to wealthy Northerners, farming, and carrying mail, the Colonel was able to support his family.

At one time the Rutledges' ancestors had owned the

plantations of Waterhon, Elmwood, and Harrietta, but as a result of the war, portions were sold off until they held only Hampton.

In spite of the fact that the splendor of plantation life had passed, visitors to Hampton were always treated royally.

Once when Archie slipped into the pantry, Martha Alston, the cook, yelled, "Don't you take nothin'! You know that's the unexpected company shelf."

After the war, too, the freeing of slaves had dislocated the agricultural system of the South. Now the twenty Negro families who remained at Hampton lived in the old slave quarters.

At the time of Archie's birth the plantation owners had summer homes to which they moved their families for three months of each year. Because of malaria and swamp fevers, the plantations were not considered healthful.

The Rutledges' summer home was in McClellanville, about ten miles from Hampton Plantation and forty miles north of Charleston. Since "The Village," as it was called, was located on salt water, it was considered to have a more healthful climate.

It was here at the "Summer Place" along Jeremy Creek that Archibald Hamilton Rutledge, the fifth of six children, was born on October 23, 1883. The little house of his birth was built of logs by his father around 1870.

Of all the children, it seemed to Archie's parents that this child had a strange wildness about him that made him one with the whistling willets, the great wood ibis, and the curlews calling across the marshes. Often he would disappear for hours without anyone's knowing where he was.

He might be watching the chimney swift, a common

summer resident of the cavernous old chimneys of Hampton. The great wings of this bird with hardly any feet fascinated Archie. He loved to watch him fly - now high, now low - with tireless energy. At last when the swift was ready to make his nest, he would snap dead twigs in flight to build a cradle in a chimney.

Since Archie had always heard of how his family had been ruined by the war, he never had an interest in playing army as most children. To him the military, uniforms, medals and ribbons, brass balls - all were trappings of death. In spite of these feelings, he did later attend a military school at the insistence of his parents.

Once Archibald shocked his father by asking, "Why are men given medals for killing other men? Have you ever killed a man?"

"The medals are given for service to one's country," his father had answered, "and, yes, I have killed some men in war."

"I am sorry for their mothers," Archie said.

The Colonel looked at Archie aghast and then turned to his wife. "Our youngest son asks me puzzling and petrifying questions," he said.

At this young age Archie harbored two desires: He wanted to be a doctor because of the stories his mother read to him about Indian healing, and he prayed that he might be a singer.

Although he never became a singer in the usual sense of the word, he did become a minstrel singing of the beauty of nature.

Except for his mother, the members of Archibald's family viewed his literary ambitions as just another peculiarity of Archibald's already eccentric character. Still, he wasn't sure of his mother's tone of laughter as she told of his first literary efforts when he was three. He had run in from outdoors and recited:

I saw a little rattlesnake
Too young to make his rattles shake.

As a matter of fact, Archie did not feel appreciated in many ways. He and his grandmother, Caroline Pinckney, who lived at Eldorado Plantation, never had very much in common.

"Archie," she would ask in her stately manner, "must you chase my poor cat up and down the stairs?"

Then she would take him by the hand and lead him to a large cedar chest gracing one side of the ballroom. There she would show him the glittering sword and ornate uniform that General Charles Cotesworth Pinckney had worn as Ambassador to the Court of St. James.

"Now," she would say, "if you want to grow up to be somebody, you must not spend your time chasing cats."

Secretly Archie was far more interested in the rack of a great chestnut-colored stag that hung on the wall. The massive antlers carried twelve points.

Fortunately for Archie, the Colonel did not agree with the young boy's grandmother. He often assuaged Archie's restless spirit with a rollicking hunt tune.

When Archie was eight, his father took him to Charleston to visit relatives. They started by horse and buggy at daylight one cold January morn and traveled all day on the Georgetown-Charleston road that in places had sand a foot deep. Arriving at Mount Pleasant at nightfall, they left their horse and buggy with a German storekeeper and walked down the long wharf to a ferry slip to take a boat for Charleston.

The ferry was guided by a cable stretched from a tree on the opposite shore a mile away. Negroes propelled the boat by grabbing hold of the cable attached to the bow of the boat and pulling it to the back of the ferry.

Archie found the bilgy old hulk frightening, as long rows of water barrels were rolled around to help steady the teetering deck.

The great harbor of Charleston looked vast and sinister to the country boy, and the mysterious city with shimmering lights was like a mirage.

Archie would never reminisce about this visit to Charleston without recalling how uncomfortable his new clothes were. He was made all the more uncomfortable when he reached his relatives' home. Maiden aunts constantly corrected his pronunciation. Even cousins of his own age scorned him for his plantation way of speaking. They laughed when Archie, knowing nothing of city life, was terrified by the sight of a policeman.

Although he found the horse-drawn street cars magical, Archie finally retreated to the high-walled garden, where he made friends with an old dog.

Charleston was entirely different from the world Archie knew, and he longed to be away from the critical eye of relatives and back with the plantation Negroes, the cattle, horses, dogs, and beautiful creatures of the woods.

Although at this time there were no trains, automobiles, or telephones at Hampton, Archie loved it. In many ways life there was like that of the early frontier.

He loved the ebb and flow of the tides as the sea winds brought their salty freshness up the creeks. Even then he knew that the mysterious delta and its wildlife would forever draw him homeward.

Three

During Archie's early years, it seemed he could never breathe enough of the wildness and beauty of nature. The magic of it all was in his blood: the birds, the animals, strange reptiles, and all the lovely mystery of the river and woods and swamp.

Hating for a day to end and force him indoors, Archie dashed back outside one evening after dinner. A pink sky lingered behind the live oaks and tall pines as Archie, surging with life, ran barefoot down the shrub-bordered pathway leading to the creek.

It was dusky there in the twilight. He checked his speed and was about to turn back when he spied a small log lying across his path.

Archie had stepped up on the log to see if he could balance himself when he felt a strange sensation. The log was giving beneath his weight. It felt even more peculiar to his bare feet.

Suddenly a writhe and a hiss sent him tearing back up the path toward the lights of the house. The fright was so great that he never told a soul.

In spite of his close calls, Archie resented anything that took him away from this outdoor life even for an hour.

So it was when the two younger Rutledge boys heard the bishop was coming. Neither Archie nor Hugh was sure just what a bishop was, but from the conversation of the grownups the boys gathered they were to experience some kind of ordeal that involved dressing up.

When their mother took two white shirts with big starched collars from the great mahogany wardrobe and laid these alongside two new black velvet suits, new shoes, and stockings, their doubts were confirmed.

On Sunday the bishop would make his annual visit to their church to preach, baptize all the babies who had been born since he paid his visit the previous year, and confirm all the boys and girls who were of confirmation age.

Because the roads were bad and buggies often in need of repair, few services were held in St. James church, making this an especially important event.

Afterwards, the bishop would come home with the Rutledges to have dinner in the large dining room of Hampton Plantation.

When the inevitable day came, Hugh and Archie were dressed in their finery and told to keep themselves spotless while last-minute details were looked after.

Far more restless than grave, quiet Hugh, Archie wandered out on the spacious front porch to wait for the family. For a time he stood there marveling at the beauty of an April morning washed fresh in last night's torrential rainfall. The trees and shrubs sparkled with cleanliness under the bright sunlight. Here and there rain lay puddled.

Thoughtful Hugh, whom Archie later said was his "balance wheel," came to stand beside him.

About that time Prince, wet, bedraggled, and happy, rounded the corner of the sprawling porch.

Seeing his playmates, he came to an abrupt halt as if he had slammed on brakes. "Listen to dat!" he grinned.

From somewhere behind the stableyard frogs croaked.

"Des 'bout a thousand. Les ketch 'em."

"We can't," Hugh spoke up, "not in these clothes."

"But a thousand," Archie moaned. "Les just go look at 'em."

With that Archie and Prince struck out toward the wet, boggy field where last night's rain had formed a pond. As Prince promised, heads of croaking frogs thickly dotted the tawny water collected in the lower part of the field.

Archie leaned down to grab a frog at the edge.

"But you said we were just coming to look." Until Hugh spoke, Archie had not realized his brother had followed.

Prince had grabbed a burlap sack from the stable, and now he stood wide-eyed, holding it open for the catch.

In a moment Hugh, too, could not resist. It seemed the best frogs were in deeper water, luring the boys out farther and farther.

Everytime they grabbed a big one, they had to make another sloshing trip back to Prince, who was grinning over the slimy, kicking collection.

Archie was standing in the middle of the pond when he looked up to see a curious expression spreading over Hugh's face. A quick glance toward Prince showed only a deserted burlap sack with frogs jumping gaily from it.

On the shore of the pond stood the Colonel.

A little while later as their clothes dried and the brothers sniffed by a bedroom window, they heard

Archie (left) and Hugh Rutledge in 1890.

Prince getting his in the kitchen.

After such a reprimand for doing wrong, the boys were strangely good for a while. They even refused to shoot an old half-wild cat with their slingshots. Of course the cat was near the plantation graveyard, and everyone knew phantoms waited for little boys who tormented cats.

Even the thought of punishment, however, did not keep Archie from scouring the plantation for adventure.

Once when he was following a Negro as he plowed a field, Archie saw him uncover an unexploded shell. He persuaded the farm hand to let him have the shell so that he and a cousin could bury it at Eldorado Plantation.

The summer he was eight, Archie shot and killed a mad dog that had terrified the whole village.

Another time he climbed down into a mossy well to put a slip knot over the head of a rattlesnake that was ruining the water in a neighbor's well.

Archie's early education, as was the other Rutledge children's, was taken care of by his mother. As a girl Margaret Seabrook had read over a hundred classics, and for a time had served as a governess for a wealthy family in London.

When Archie was old enough, he rode a horse to school along a narrow, sandy road to a plantation several miles away. Hugh rode Redbird and Archie Rocket.

The brothers rarely followed the road but wound in and out of the old woodpaths through the wildwoods. It was here that Archie learned much of nature. He loved this ride although it was not without pitfalls.

One morning a dog jumped from some bushes at the young riders. Frightened, their mounts reared violently and crashed into the thicket of young pines across the road.

Hugh managed to stay astride his mount, but Rocket rushed Archie against a pine that scraped him beneath the horse's feet. He suffered a gash on his head and some broken ribs.

Rocket ran without his rider while Hugh pulled his younger brother up behind him and took him home. It was three weeks before Archie could return to school.

Another time a stray bull attacked them.

In spite of their obstacles, Hugh usually made it to school on time, but Archie rarely did. Sometimes he lagged behind to watch a flock of wild turkeys. He wondered at the way they taxied before they took off to fly.

And no matter how many times he passed the great Peachtree Oak at the plantation home of Thomas Lynch, Jr., a signer of the Declaration of Independence, the tree still fascinated him.

Much to Archie's dismay, he could never keep the schoolroom door from squeaking when he made an effort to slip his slender frame through the door and into his desk. Always a sea of faces turned toward him.

Miss Anne Ashburn Lucas, usually the patient teacher, never failed to question. "What was it this time 'Wilful Archie'? Were you following a bird, or was it necessary for you to kill a rattler that crossed your path?"

Archie didn't mind the name his teacher had coined for him. He knew he had the reputation for being the most inquisitive and restless student in Miss Lucas' class. Too, he had often heard his mother say he got his tardiness from his father.

"Margaret," the Colonel would say, "I'm late for supper, but I was on time to see those mallards coming in over the delta fields."

Another time his father's lateness might be due to his lingering to admire wild roses along a dusty roadside, a tiny green fern, or the spring song of a parula warbler.

Archie's father never reprimanded him for being late, for he believed in a gentle and leisurely existence. Often he sat on the wide veranda in his favorite hickory rocking chair, his hand drooping down to stroke the ears of a hound puppy.

"The wild things in nature rarely hurry unless they

are in danger," he would say. "How can life be rich if we dash through it?"

Once Archie had found his father sitting in the garden enjoying the balmy sunshine of a spring morning. Seeing his young son, the Colonel called him to come sit beside him.

"People think I'm lazy," he confessed, "but I just hate to waste beautiful time working. Besides, hurrying shows a lack of poise."

Painstakingly the Colonel would identify for Archie flowers and shrubs. "I would rather walk than ride. Then if I see a tree, I can tell whether it is a red oak, whether a shout is a neighbor's greeting or the braying of a jackass. Yes," he continued, "speed will take you somewhere, but when you have arrived, that's all you can say."

No doubt Miss Lucas had discussed Archie's habitual tardiness with his mother and had become resigned to it. Yet she in her teacherlike manner always scolded him. The really bad part about it as far as Archie was concerned was that pretty Alice Lucas heard him get fussed at, and from her own sister, too.

It was indeed hard to concentrate on studies when just outside those windows lay a boy's paradise. How he longed to climb to the crotch of a bay tree and watch wildlife. Hidden by jessamine vines draping the trees, he loved to imitate the songs of certain birds or the cries of beasts.

The sounds of early morning on the plantation - the Negroes driving teams of mules and oxen to the fields, the lowing of the cattle in the stableyard, the calling of the quail, cardinals, and orchard orioles - all were far more enticing than the classroom.

Being wise in the ways of the woods intrigued Archie more than a lesson in mathematics.

Four

In the summer of 1893 when Archie was almost ten, he experienced his first great sorrow. As usual, the Rutledges were spending the hottest part of the year in the mountains south of Asheville, North Carolina.

To offset expenses for the journey to and from the mountains, the Rutledges took in boarders at their summer home near Flat Rock. It was here that Archie's brother Hugh suffered a fatal accident. Quiet, thoughtful Hugh had always been such a contrast to restless Archie.

On this late afternoon the boys were making their daily trek to the post office. They used the route they loved best - the railroad track.

Happily they walked the rails with arms outstretched for balancing, or jumped from one tarry crosstie to another with great puffs of energy.

No sound of an oncoming train marred the freedom they felt on the tracks. Thus they were unaware that just around the sharp bend ahead a train had stopped for an auxiliary engine.

Not until they saw it whirling backwards toward them at terrific speed did they realize the impending danger.

Archie jumped free of the tracks, but the pounding wheels caught Hugh.

Pulling his brother's body from beneath the driving steel created a trauma from which Archie would never fully recover.

When people gathered about Archie as he bent over the crushed body of his brother, he slipped away and ran the two miles up the mountain road to tell his mother and sisters.

Breathless, terrified, and covered with blood, he brought home the news of Hugh's death.

Mrs. Rutledge folded her son in her arms. Nearby, one of his distraught sisters cried out, "Oh, if it could only have been Archie instead."

It had, Archie felt, always been his fault when bad things happened, so it stood to reason that he would be blamed for his brother's death. If only he did not always do so many things that called for scolding. It had always seemed to Archie that he needed to do something to prove himself. His brothers and sisters seemed to "belong," but he did not - or so he thought. In his grief he remembered that once even Hugh had complained about him. "Archie will keep on doing things," he had said.

Stepping out into the twilight of the woods, he wept. How could he live all of his life without Hugh?

Even though Archie knew that his sister's words were said in a moment of grief, he was to be haunted by them for the rest of his life.

Yet, in a sense, his sister's cutting remark was an inspiration. As the deep wound of losing Hugh began to heal, Archie resolved to make his family proud of him.

As hard as he tried, though, he did not like to study

his lessons. Every waking moment was spent in the fields, woods, on the river, or the delta. The magic and mystery of the outdoors drew him as if magnets lay buried there. Sometimes he did not even realize where his feet were carrying him.

At night Archie did as other members of his family and visitors - as there were always relatives at Hampton - he read. Sometimes his mother or one of his aunts read aloud to the group. Sir Walter Scott was his favorite. Still, he could never quite understand why knights would ride forth alone, longing to meet someone they could kill. He thought this a disgusting way to spend one's time and strength. It would be far more noble, he felt, to let them live.

Another favorite was Edgar Allan Poe, even though his weird tales sometimes made Archie afraid of the night. Once he selected a French novel he had seen someone else take from the bookcases lining the wall. It was somewhat sexy, but since he knew little of such things, he laid it aside. In its place he read Scott's "Lady of the Lake."

Countless hours of Archie's life, however, were spent watching wild animals. A half mile from Hampton lay a little pond choked by alders, wild blackberries, and masses of tangled muscadine vines. This shimmering water, connected to the Santee River by an almost hidden watercourse, was a favorite spot for Archie.

Occasionally he would see an otter come into the pond from the river. Archie watched the furry little animal glide in and out of the black water among the cypress knees. The otter, not realizing he had an audience, would lie on his favorite log and preen his fur.

Still in hiding, Archie watched the otter enjoy his moments of relaxation and appreciation of the beauty about him before he darted in a soft foamy plunge beneath the roots of an immense cypress to his den.

Still, for a plantation boy there was much responsibility. One of Archie's jobs involved riding for the mail. The post office was seven miles from Hampton Plantation, and there was no rural delivery. The mail did not reach the local post office until late in the evening. At an early age Archie began to meet the mail delivery, leaving at twilight and returning after nightfall.

He liked the concert of frogs he often heard along the way, especially if there was a promise of rain. Sometimes he would rein his horse to listen to their piping **Knee-deep! Knee-deep!** And the shrill sopranos joining with **Thigh-high! Thigh-high!**

His return trip in eerie starlight or pitch darkness was not always so enjoyable. Once he heard a wild cat scream. Even without sounds, the bushes took on haunting shapes, filling him with a mixture of dread, wonder, and fear. Already his mind was confused with stories of "hants" and bats as big as a turkey.

Although Archie's experiences as a night rider, along with the stillness and loneliness, were often frightening, they made a deep impression on him.

And then it was Archie's duty to care for the expectant mothers among the plantation's cows, goats, and hogs. This was a meaningful responsibility, as Archie had always been such a careful observer of the love between mother and child in domestic and wild animals.

He learned early that a mother, whether wild or tame, will savagely defend her young. Sallie, a great sow on the plantation, developed an unusual secretiveness. Knowing it must be time for her young, Archie followed her to a wild, blossomy thicket on Sam Hill, where he peered at her from behind dense pine boughs.

When she had chosen a suitable place, old Sallie set about preparing her home for her little pigs. The sow's attitude and behavior touched Archie as he watched her ready the tiny area. She had chosen a spot flanked by thick myrtle bushes, and now she made her bedding by pushing together pinestraw and leaves. Archie marveled that she made the north and west sides heavier than she did the others.

At dusk he finally slipped away, leaving Sallie in her newly made home.

The next morning just after breakfast Archie started toward Sam Hill. As usual, he carried his gun. This time it was to shoot at crows that were pulling up young corn.

When he was still a good way off, he noticed turkey buzzards circling low over the very spot where Sallie had made her bed. He quickened his pace, for he could already see that some of the arrogant creatures were settling down.

Archie knew that vultures could tell that Sallie was weak at this time and would be unable to defend her brood. He thought of the day he had lain motionless on the warm sand at Bull's Island trying to attract some circling buzzards. He had watched them through one partly opened eye, but he could not fool them. Somehow they knew that he was not disabled or dead.

Faint squeals and a pathetic, though coarse, protest emerged from old Sallie's bed. One look through the bushes and Archie realized what was happening. The vultures were trying to take the sow's new-born babies. Sallie stood with her broad back against the thickest part of the bed. Beneath her heaving flanks, Archie could see her trembling brood. Sallie's eyes gleamed; her head reared backwards; and she champed her great jaws vengefully. Every few moments one of the big black-winged birds would swoop down toward the pigs.

Archie aimed his gun and pulled the trigger. The

turkey buzzards scattered to the highest limbs of the surrounding trees.

For days Archie continued to watch after Sallie until she was stronger. Then he led her and her babies to the barn, where she raised her young until they could take care of themselves.

Just as Archie learned that a mother animal is loyal to her young, he learned that the baby animal is obedient to its mother. A turpentine worker gave him a tiny fawn he found in the woods. It was so young and wobbly that it could take just a few steps on its tiny hoofs. Archie decided to make a pet of it. Every day he fed it with a bottle of milk. As the fawn became stronger, Archie began to lay it in a patch of oats. At night when he went to bring it in, he noticed the little animal was lying in the same spot as he had left it.

Archie told his mother about his strange fawn who would lie curled up snugly in the oats all day.

"You see, Archie," his mother, who was also a lover of nature, explained, "in the short time the fawn was with his mother in the woods, she taught him to stay where she put him when she left to go away to feed. It was being obedient."

Thereafter Archie took special notice of mothers and their children. Once he saw the nest a wild rabbit had made cozy for her babies by pulling fur from her breast and lining the grass with it.

On one of the many days when Archie was riding with the Colonel after stock, they came to a dense thicket of springtime greenery. Hearing a noise in some nearby myrtles, they stopped their horses.

Whatever had moved now stood motionless. Then a doe stole from behind a myrtle bush. She did not see the riders but cocked her head to listen. Just behind her a tiny fawn swayed and teetered on delicate legs.

Once more the mother tilted her head, one ear forward, one backwards. In childish fashion the fawn started to frisk. To Archie's surprise, the mother lifted her foreleg, set her foot lightly on the back of the fawn and pressed him gently into the warm brown grass.

All remained quiet until Archie's horse stamped his foot. At once the doe moved through the myrtle, being careful to adjust her speed to the pace of her fawn.

Thereafter, Archie took note that it was easy to walk up to a crouched fawn because he remains still in obedience to the mother who left him there.

Yet another duty of Archie's was to cross the river just behind their home to round up and feed the half-wild stock the family pastured on one of the islands of the delta.

He liked to paddle his canoe down the creek. Occasionally there would be a great blue heron waiting to pierce a fish with its spearlike beak. In the late afternoon wood ducks would come flocking into the old fields of the delta from their daytime haunts in the swamps and ponds of the deep pinelands.

A great bald cypress tree was Archie's favorite place from which to watch the ducks. No matter where they were headed, they always flew over that cypress. Archie would become so fascinated with the way the mothers would lead their streaming broods that he often stayed until after sundown.

Heading home in the dim goblin night, Archie would hear the flit of a fairy's wing or an elfin chuckle from a knob-headed gnome. Always this gave him a strange mixture of fear and pleasure.

Five

For longer than Archie could remember he had begged his father to take him deer hunting. Already Archie knew the names and locations of deer stands. He knew, too, that hunters of long ago had given these stands names like Shirttail Stand, Doeboy, and Handkerchief after some triumph or disaster that had occurred there. Others like old L.P.'s Stand and Morgan's Stand had taken their names from a particular hunter.

It had always seemed strange yet wonderful to Archie that deer used the same crossings year after year. He understood that because deer habitually go along the same routes, that those places are called "deer crossings," and it was at these places a hunter would "stand" to wait for the deer.

All the hunters favored Log Landing, as that was a routine place for deer to take off to swim the river by Hampton Plantation.

A born woodsman, the Colonel had primed his son with many tales of his own deer hunts. Once he had shown Archie the very spot of a memorable experience.

"Now here, Son," he had said, "a huge ten-point stag stepped across the road and vanished."

"How do you know it wasn't a doe?" Archie had asked.

"A buck walks heavily and is blunt-toed," his father answered. "You might say he wears a number ten shoe."

Archie would watch the smile lines around his father's eyes as he continued. "Now a doe is a lady. She minces along in high-heeled slippers."

One afternoon while Archie and his father were walking along a riverbank, the Colonel pointed to a wild grapevine that hung in a loop above the black water.

"Once," he said, "a deer I had wounded ran three miles to this river, and when I got here, I found him captured by this very vine."

"Did you get him?" Archie questioned.

"You know, Son, he made such a great race that I felt sorry for him. I took out my knife and cut him free."

Archie could understand his father's feelings, and momentarily he had a pang of guilt about the way he had pestered the little mud dauber and even the old bulls on the plantation.

"Oh, hunting is a great sport," the Colonel continued, "but it's often a greater sport to see a gallant wild thing get away."

With his elder brothers and sisters away at boarding school, life held many solitary hours for Archie. Now that he was going on ten, his urge to go deer hunting was stronger than ever.

Seeing the tall figure of his father seated on the porch, Archie saw him surreptitiously thrust something in his pocket.

"What do you have?" he asked in his childlike,

brazen manner. "What did you put in your pocket?"

His father slowly drew out a faded photograph of Hugh. Archie saw tears in his father's eyes as he pulled him onto his lap. In one of his rare moments of genuine tenderness he put his strong arms around his son.

This shared grief led to his father's giving to Archie the best gift that anyone can give another - himself. Knowing Archie's loneliness, the Colonel gave the boy more comradeship and at the same time helped to comfort himself over his own loss.

The Colonel had always been proud of the way Archie handled a gun, and now at last he promised to take him deer hunting. Archie's feeling of happiness was mixed with that of anxiety. What if things did not turn out the way he had dreamed they would? What if he let his deer get away? That could very well happen with the gun he would be using. He owned only a little single-barrel, and it had a very short barrel at that. Worst of all, the barrel had a slight bend in it.

The secret of how the bend got there was known only to Archie and to one other person. He had been crawling after some doves in a corn field when he had accidently thrust the muzzle into the earth.

A moment later, without knowing the barrel had been choked with dirt, he fired. The shot kicked him flat and burst open the end of his gun like a lily.

Shamefaced, Archie had carried the gun home, all the while wondering how he would hide it - this symbol of his immaturity.

Luckily the plantation blacksmith had seen it. "I'll fix that gun for you in no time at all," he had said. In his shop, which smelled of coal and hot metal, he had filed the end and smoothed it down.

Now when Archie sighted, he had learned to make allowances for the bend. That was all right against

Archie's father, Col. Henry Middleton Rutledge II, a born woodsman, took him on his first deer hunt.

doves or other birds in flight. But a deer?

Archie tried to concentrate on what his father had told him about letting the brave buck escape. Perhaps he would not think it too bad if Archie let one get away. Still . . . .

On the morning of the hunt Archie's stomach churned with excitement and fear. How many times had he heard his father say that there was no grander sport in the whole world than bringing down a deer?

At last the moment of crisis arrived. Once in the woods, each hunter was given a stand. Filled with anxiety, Archie stood at his. He stared so hard at the "drive" that the trees seemed to be coming toward him.

Every shadow of light, every movement in the woods came alive: towhee rustled dead leaves; a tiny warbler trembled on a branch; a crow cawed from a distance; a hawk circled above the pines. But there was no sign of a deer.

After what seemed forever, a Negro "driver" began to whoop and whistle to the dogs. Still nothing. Not even a sound from the dogs.

At last a hound struck up a bark and Archie's heart began to hammer. Shortly, though, the Negro whistled the dog off and Archie could hear the driver splashing into pools of water. Once he saw sunlight on the barrel of a gun.

For a quick moment Archie glanced at a nearby pond. A blue heron stood like a statue in the dark water.

When he looked back toward the drive, not three hundred yards away, a splendid buck parted the bay bushes. Above a shaggy black chest great antlers glinted in the sunlight.

The dogs opened a full cry, and with a single bound the buck cleared the thicket and headed straight for Archie.

Archie remembered his father's warning never to follow a deer with his gun but to pick an open space between two pines and shoot the moment the deer darkened it. He leveled his damaged gun on an aperture between two giant short-leafed pines.

Suddenly the great buck lunged in front of the gun. Archie fired.

Through the smoke from his gun he saw the deer in flight. Then the dogs passed him like a whirlwind.

In moments two old hunters came riding up. "Dat's de grandpa buck, Cap'n," the driver said. "I hope you done shot him."

But there was no hope in his voice as he dismounted and began looking on the ground for the bloodstains.

Then he cried out and fell to his knees in the pinestraw. "You hit dat grandpa! You hit dat grandpa!"

"But where are the dogs?" Archie asked, just as his father joined the group. "I can't hear them."

They listened and the silence spread until the Colonel said, "They must have overthrown the buck."

A few minutes later they found the buck stone dead with the hounds standing guard over him. Behind the foreshoulder were three buckshot wounds.

The pride that the Colonel showed over his son's feat delighted Archie. It always seemed to him that after the deer hunt his father felt he had found in his son someone who could carry on the plantation's tradition of sport. To the end of his days the Colonel considered the taking of a whitetail stag an accomplishment of distinction.

As for Archie, he knew beyond a shadow of a doubt that he would not trade places with his city cousins for all the world.

Six

Losing Hugh brought Archie closer not only to his father but to Tom, his next older brother.

Whenever Tom was not away in boarding school, he allowed his young brother to do things with him. There were always alligators to try to capture, wood ducks to shoot by the river and in the pine-woods ponds, or perch and black bass to catch in the rice field canals. Too, they rambled, most often with Prince, through the thickets in search of blueberries, fox grapes, and thick-skinned muscadines.

On occasion whenever the Colonel had to go into Charleston on business, he would put Tom in charge of certain plantation chores. This included overseeing the feeding of stock, laying in of the daily supply of firewood, and distributing groceries from the commissary to the workers.

Their smaller duties included feeding the chickens and turkeys, which required little attention because so much rice and corn lay waste around the barnyard and feed house.

Tom was tending the fowl, with Archie and Prince close by, when Red Lightning, their father's prize gamecock, strutted by arrogantly.

"Say," Tom said, "let's take Red Lightning over to that common rooster everybody hates in the 'street' and let Red Lightning teach him a thing or two."

"Yeah," added Prince, "he the one that scratch up my peanut vines."

"Just last week," Tom went on, "he made me lose that flock of crows I was crawling after. Anyway, everybody's sick of his racket."

"Well -" Archie began, "I don't hate him enough to see him killed."

But Tom was already planning. "Arch, you be Red's second, and Prince can hold the sponge for the other one. I'm going to watch to be sure the fight is fair. And," he went on excitedly, "we really ought to give that lowbred fellow a handicap; I know he'll faint when he sees Red's spurs."

As Tom talked, he assured Prince and Archie that there would be no actual fight. His purpose was not to injure the common rooster but to humiliate him and teach him a lesson.

The whole idea began to appear alluring and straight away Archie coaxed Red Lightning to his feet. Three years earlier the Colonel had acquired the rooster from western North Carolina where the renown strain of Fletcher games had originated, and he was known as the most beautiful gamecock in the countryside.

Picking up Red Lightning, Archie was again impressed with his regal splendor. The finely shaped head was perfectly patterned in dark red and black feathers. His legs were like a race horse's in shape and symmetry, and his tail feathers a triumph of color.

Prince ran ahead to the "street," as the area where

the Negroes lived was called, to locate the common rooster. Meanwhile, Tom and Archie, with Red Lightning tucked under Archie's arm, made their way across the abandoned rice bank near the river.

In moments Prince dashed back to meet them with a wide grin. He had seen the enemy and was ready to lead them to it.

As the boys came upon the gawky old rooster scratching in the clearing for his hens, they had a moment of misgiving.

"I wish," Tom confessed, "that he looked more like a fighter."

Archie, holding the gamecock in front of him, cautiously approached the dirty-white rooster. At a distance of about six feet, he dropped Red Lightning. The proud cock landed on his spread spurs, bent himself backward, and let out a mighty crow from his splendid throat.

At that moment Prince's rooster lit out toward Red Lightning and struck him with the full fury of his strength.

Shocked, Red Lightning sprawled backward. Somewhat dazed and disheveled, he arose, ruffled his neck feathers forward, and stared at his opponent.

The boys drew closer.

Red Lightning seemed to have caught on. He sprang into the air to drive his spurs into this opponent's head. But the old rooster ducked and whirled, and before Red Lightning could recover, struck him a terrific blow. Then with his spurs, wings, and body he began to buffet Red Lightning.

The boys watched in amazement as Red Lightning looked about nervously, turned, and fled.

The common rooster streaked in hot pursuit.

Prince bent over in laughter, but Tom and Arch were

mortified. Never did they dream the plantation's prize rooster had a yellow feather.

In the distance they could hear the sqawks of a rooster taking a good whipping. They hurried toward the squawking, hoping as they ran that the tide had turned.

Through broomsedge and across a muddy ditch they ran until they spied Red Lightning with the front half of his body jammed under a trash-choked bank. Behind him the common rooster reined blow after blow. Beautiful red and black feathers lay all about. Several drifted in the murky stream.

Tom jumped down into the ditch, landing with a splash in the mud and water. Prince and Archie watched as he made an angry pass at the common rooster, who avoided his blow, beat his wings, and crowed.

Bending down, Tom pulled Red Lightning from his hiding place. He looked bedraggled, frightened, and bruised.

When Tom had struggled up the bank with him, the three examined him for injuries. Most of his tail feathers were gone; his back was marked with cuts of blunt spurs; and what feathers had not been broken and torn out were plastered in mud. Worse still, he had lost the courageous air expected of a rooster of his breeding.

"He'll never look the same again," Archie wailed.

"And yo' Pa loved dat rooster so!" cried Prince.

The brothers had no intention of letting the Colonel know of their escapade. Now it would be impossible to keep it from him.

As they trudged home, with Tom carrying Red Lightning, Archie knew his brother's thoughts were his own. Would their father ever again trust them to keep the plantation in his absence? What they had done involved not only trustworthiness but honor.

Hours later, their father sat telling them of his journey to Charleston. He seemed so frank and open-hearted. Archie looked at Tom. The look Tom returned showed that he, too, felt mean and untrustworthy.

Finally they could bear their burden no longer.

When they had told the Colonel all, he looked at his sons with a smile so gentle it was painful.

"The game," he said, "will be all right in a week or so, and will be as pretty as ever after the first moulting. I am not worried about him, but you boys must never fight chickens again."

"Besides," he went on, "I would have told you Red Lightning would not fight. Fletcher had a strain of what he called 'tame' games, and I got him to pick me one. Red Lightning has the look and carriage of a fighter but he's no fighter. I'm glad because fighting is never a sport."

The boys hung their heads as he added, "There are too many clean sports, especially here on the plantation, for you to resort to bullyragging a pair of roosters."

Seven

Archie and Prince Alston prided themselves on knowing each other pretty well. They had been born about the same time, and since Martha Alston was the Rutledges' cook, she always brought her young son with her.

Thus, the boys became inseparable playmates. Whatever happened to one, happened to the other. Before they were five the same dog had bitten them, the same black goat had butted them, they had been thrown from the same pony, and the Colonel had whipped them both for the same kind of mischief.

Not only did the boys pride themselves on knowing each other but on knowing the various personalities of the animals on the plantation. However, a yoke of oxen named Cain and Abel completely escaped their understanding.

The boys knew that bulls were considered dangerous and that a cow with a young calf may not be friendly. They knew, too, that an ox was a symbol of pastoral peace.

It turned out, though, that none of this was true of Abel. Unlike the biblical character, this Abel was downright wicked. The Negroes looked upon him with a great deal of distrust and a little bit of superstitious dread.

The only Negro who took up for the wicked creature was Prince. When Abel was mentioned, Prince always commented, "He just ugly." Then he would laugh and add. "He can't hep how he look."

In spite of Prince's judgment, everybody, as well as all the cattle, feared Abel. Just recently he had rushed a young steer against the straw rick and gored him.

Because plantation fields were vast, the fences separating them lay far apart. Heavy thickets grew along the banks of the ditches, allowing an animal such as Abel to browse unnoticed until someone came face to face with him.

It was one of the plantation fears that someday Big Abel would catch a person and corner him. If this should happen on a small farm, help might be within call, but not on a plantation. Some hands might be far out in the pine woods, dipping turpentine or splitting rails; others could be down in the rice fields or across on the island. Woe unto the person Abel cornered.

Late one afternoon Archie and Prince were at the stable lot, the liveliest place on the plantation at that time of day.

Brother Tom helped with the feeding of the horses and the milking of the cows, while the hogs fought and squealed over their share of rice flour and sweet potatoes.

In winter the Colonel always let all the wild hogs and stray cattle come up from the woods and into the enclosure to spend cold nights beside the big rick, or covered rack of straw, in the middle of the fenced-in area. There they could not only take shelter against the wind but they could feed, for the woods offered them little during winter.

Abel was the conqueror of all newcomers. He even battled a large bull, who thereafter withdrew to the windy end of the rick.

Prince was in the stable loft pushing down hay for the horses. His father Will was milking a cow in the stall below him.

Tom and Archie heard Will say to nobody in particular. "Dat Big Abel is a mean ox."

Then they heard Prince chuckle. "I don't 'fraid him. Abel and Prince be friends ever since hatchet was a hammer."

"Yeah," Will answered, "some of these days he's gwine hammer you."

When Prince came down from the loft, Tom called him over.

"What do you say we tackle old Abel tonight?" Tom asked in a low voice.

"Tackle him?" Prince questioned.

"We want to find out," Archie explained, "whether he's bad or not. We know you're not afraid of him, and we need your help."

"Abel's all right," Prince said, "but his horns is mighty long."

"We thought maybe you could get a rope around his horns for us," Tom continued. "Then we could get him up close to the fence and try to ride him."

"Ride Abel?" Prince's eyes widened. "I wouldn't ride dat oxen if I neber ride agin!"

"Can you just get a rope over his horns?" Archie persisted.

Prince nodded his head, went into a small log outbuilding nearby and brought out a weathered gray plow line in which he tied a slip knot at the end.

Before long the three fellows climbed the fence and crossed the little "hog crawl" that separated the stable lot proper from the large enclosure where the big rick and all the cattle were.

Some of the cattle ran out of the gate when they saw the boys; others stopped feeding and eyed them with distrust, but Big Abel did not even give them a glance.

The indifference of the great animal with scythe-like horns affected the boys worse than open hostility would have.

Tom and Archie stopped at the bars, but Prince, carrying the rope, slipped quietly into the lot and walked up to Big Abel.

He ran his hand over the huge ox's side, stroked his neck, and set the noose over the horns.

Much to the amazement of the others, Prince then led Abel up to the bars and, crawling through, handed Archie the rope.

"Are we going to ride?" Archie's question to his older brother contained a hint of doubt.

"Prince," Tom said, "since he likes you, why don't you try him first?"

Prince shook his head. All the while Abel was looking through the bars at the boys.

Finally, Prince said, "Abel's mighty particular."

"Pshaw!" Tom exclaimed, "I'm not going to let that old fraud back me down."

With that he put one foot through the fence and stooped to get between the bars.

Just as Prince grabbed at Tom's coat, Abel made a lunge at Tom and one of his sharp horns scraped against the rail.

Big Abel snorted, lowered his head, and spread his legs.

The plantation Negroes, returning home through the twilight, began to gather to see what was going on.

This put a different light on things. Now Tom and Archie felt that, having collected a crowd, they were bound to give them some entertainment.

Old Isaac, one of the plantation sages, edged near the fence and peered through at the ox.

"That Abel," he said, "takes his name from the Bible, but his meanness come from the debil. What you gwine do to him, Mas' Tom?"

"We don't know exactly," Tom answered, the indecision registering in his voice.

Before Archie knew it, he heard himself say, "Here, Prince, hold the rope, I'm gonna beat old Abel to the straw rick."

Archie was already crawling through the bars. "Just let me get clear," he was saying, "and then turn him loose, and I'll show you a race."

Archie heard murmurs go through the watching Negroes, and he was about to call to Prince to let Abel free when the ox broke loose and wheeled on him.

Abel was so quick that he came near hooking Archie with a sweep of his horns.

Archie had a fleeting glimpse of the horror on the faces on the other side of the fence and of Prince's struggling to get through the bars to grab the rope.

Knowing he'd never get back through the fence, Archie scrambled for the only spot of safety - the straw rick thirty yards away.

Moments ahead of Abel, Archie grabbed a stout hickory stave on the rick, pulled himself up, and fell panting onto the straw.

It was almost dark now, and even though Archie was out of danger temporarily, he could not get down and out of the fence. His tormentor stood watch beneath him, looking for all the world as if he remembered Archie's tickling his nostrils with a broomstraw.

"Prince!" Archie called. "Can you come and get him?"

"Abel's vexed," Prince answered, "but I'll try."

As Prince climbed through the fence, the other Negroes poked fun at him.

"Lemme hold yo' hat," one called.

"I'll tell yo' pa that I'se the last one to see you," another said.

But Prince walked straight across the stable lot toward Abel.

Looking down from his spot of refuge, Archie could not help admiring Prince's bravery.

Suddenly big Abel heard steps behind him. He whirled and with head down made straight for Prince.

Prince was so taken by surprise that for a moment he hesitated. Then he let out a scream and a threat.

Not until the animal was almost upon him did he turn and run.

Even though Prince reached the fence, Archie saw the burly head of Abel lower, then brought upward in a swift sweep that sent Prince flying over the top of the rail fence.

A lump came into Archie's throat. If he had caused Prince to get hurt—

But even in the dimness of the oncoming night, he could see Prince grinning.

When the waiting Negroes saw that Prince was not hurt, the banter picked up again.

"Wat's yo' hurry, Prince?"

"I neber knew you could fly like dat."

"Prince, Abel looking fo' you."

Now that Prince was out of reach, Abel turned his attention again to Archie atop the hay rack.

The sun was almost down now and the Negroes began to drift away to their homes. Archie knew the people at the house would be wondering what had happened.

At least Tom and Prince were still with him. They were trying to figure out some way to get Archie down from the rick and out of the stable lot when they saw the Colonel coming down the path. He had come to ask Prince to take some choice ears of corn to the foreman's house on his way home.

It was too dark for Archie to see his father's face when Tom told him of his youngest son's predicament, but Archie heard his laughter ring out.

Then he watched as the Colonel walked over to the fence and held out an ear of corn.

"Come, Abel! Come!" he called in his softest, most persuasive voice.

To the boys' surprise, the big ox obeyed.

While Abel was rolling the corn in his mouth, the Colonel took the dangling rope in his hand and hitched it around a cedar post. Then he called Archie to come down.

"Big Abel is all right," the Colonel said. "He just gets touchy when he's bothered. Anyway, you boys ought to know that an animal has no sense of humor."

Eight

Of all the creatures of the delta, the wild boar was the most fearful. Early in Archie's life he had heard a wise driver of a deer hunt tell the hunters, "If a buck comes out, shoot him; but if a wild boar comes, let him pass."

Archie learned, too, that although these wild animals can be quite large, they move with great speed. And even though they are descended from good stock, they have gone utterly wild and can be one of the meanest animals of the woods.

Some hunters, concerned for their animals as well as themselves, refuse to take a certain deer drive "because a big boar haunts that place." Likewise, few dogs, sensing the danger of being ripped by the great tusks, will take on a wild boar. Some even refuse to follow one.

The chief reason a boar is so hard to kill is his special armor. Heavy shields of callus cover his cheeks and chest.

The great forests that covered fifty miles in three directions from Hampton served as refuges for all wild animals, especially these wild boar or wild hogs.

Dense thickets of laurel-like trees, myrtle bushes, and the deep swamps and bays covered their crafty wanderings.

A few miles from the plantation a large bay of several acres had been burned off. As a result, bushes and vines had covered it more densely than ever. Because of the entanglements of thick vines and the treacherous footing, horses could not be ridden through it.

Even the hounds, who were known for going anywhere, were often baffled by the apparently endless mazes interrupted by shallow ponds.

It was at a place known as Burnt Bay that Tom, Archie, and Prince had a memorable encounter with a great white boar.

Prince first brought the news that he had seen a boar come out on a ridge not far from Burnt Bay. From the expression of his face as he told the tale, the brothers drew the conclusion that Prince was somewhat unsure of just what he had seen. His looks suggested it might have been a "hant."

The three of them stood beneath a huge live oak in the backyard of Hampton as Prince recounted his story. He described the incident in great detail. He even took a stick and sketched a crude map of Burnt Bay in the sand.

"Well, Prince," Tom challenged the younger boy. "if he is there, what are we going to do about it?"

Archie spoke up quickly. "Let's go after him. That old hound Singer will hold that hog."

Prince chuckled, but the laugh had a nervous ring.

"Oh, my," he said, "I sorry fo' ole Singer. He'll sing today like he never done sung befo'."

Already fun hung in the air.

Tom headed toward the house for buckskin thongs to

tie up the prize once they subdued him. Prince and Archie ran off to the rice barn to call up old Singer, who would be there asleep in the sun.

"Take yo' rest, po' dog," said Prince, "cause dere will be no mo' rest fo' you dis day." Prince danced a shuffle before Singer and clapped his hands. "I think you is gwine to cross Jordan today."

Singer awoke and flapped his tail on the ground without showing another trace of emotion in his body.

Archie slipped on the dog's collar and patted his head. Singer slowly pulled himself up by sections and followed along.

Joining Tom at the house, they set off with Singer down the road toward Burnt Bay.

In less than an hour the boys edged through soft yellow broomsedge. The damp sweet aroma of sphagnum moss and pine filled the air.

At the edge of the woods the three sat on a fallen log and considered the task before them. Singer lay down at their feet and fell asleep.

"Right yonder," Prince said, pointing to a little sandy ridge, "is where I done seen 'im."

"Well, Prince," Tom asked, "what do you think is the best way to go about hunting him?"

For once Prince became serious. "If we's gwine to get 'im," he answered, nodding toward the dense thicket of Burnt Bay, "we's got to go in after 'im 'cause he ain't coming out here to us."

"But what about Singer?" Archie asked, not wanting to see the old hound get gored.

"When old Singer starts to bay," Prince said, "we got to be dere."

"Could you tell if he had long tusks?" Tom asked.

Prince stretched out his arm and pulled up his sleeve. Then he measured off a distance of at least ten inches.

"Fine trophies," said Tom, getting up. "Let's make them ours."

At the edge of the bay the boys agreed to spread out and walk toward the ridge where Prince had seen the white boar.

As Archie moved ahead, stepping in quaking bogs, he thought of the time he had jumped over some oozy black water onto what he thought was a mossy hillock. Instead, it had been a huge snapping turtle. Trying to watch where he stepped, he snagged his shirt on matted branches and cringed as briars tore into his flesh.

Old Singer, who had followed him, fared better, for he nuzzled under thick brush using the secret trails made by wild creatures.

When they were about halfway to the ridge, Singer began to bark. Then quite near Archie something exploded within the myrtle bushes, shaking the bay thicket and giving off the penetrating odor of a wild hog.

Old Singer, now fully alive, dashed into the bushes, hot on his trail.

In a matter of minutes Singer's prolonged howls echoed from the thicket.

Shouting to Tom and Prince, Archie forced his way through the jungle of vines and branches. Prince had just said they must be on the spot when Singer bayed, and the woods echoed with the long, deep sounds.

Panic-stricken, Archie knew the boar would kill the hound. He couldn't wait for the others to help.

In another desperate struggle he burst through a small opening. Just the other side of a clump of bushes the two animals faced each other.

Standing in a shallow pool of water, the boar bristled. A few feet away Singer stood straddled-legged in an attempt to attack.

The boar's back was to Archie, but little good it did

him, for he had come without a weapon.

If only he could reach through the thicket separating him from the boar and catch hold of his back leg. If he could just hold on to him until the others got there.

Crouching, he slipped forward and extended his arm for the grasp.

Suddenly the boar champed his jaws and whirled like a flash. The savage head, the gleaming eyes, the fearful tusks glared at Archie through the tunnel-like opening.

At that moment old Singer gripped the boar from behind. Once more the boar whirled savagely and gave a cruel toss of his head, throwing the hound clear across the shallow pond.

The last glimpse Archie had of the grizzled hog was his flight through the brake.

Shouting to Tom and Prince, Archie waded toward Singer, who lay helpless in the bay bushes.

Archie bent over him and Singer slowly opened his eyes and beat his tail feebly.

Archie knelt in the moss and swamp ferns as he ran his hands along the dog's body to feel for wounds from the dreadful tusks.

Gently he rolled Singer over. Not a scar.

"Why, you old fraud!" he exclaimed. "You're not even hurt."

At that the hound got to his feet and shook violently, splattering Archie with muddy water.

Just then Prince and Tom broke through the thicket.

Wild-eyed, they listened to Archie's tale.

Finally, Prince chuckled. "Dat boar is de boss of dis bay."

Accepting Prince's acknowledgement, at least for the time being, they set out for the plantation with old Singer leading the way. The new-found energy of the dog baffled them.

"Mr. Singer," Prince said, "dere's no need fo' you to hold dat tail so high 'cause you ain't done nothing but lost yo' breath."

After that day when the boys had nothing much to do, Prince would say, "Let's go catch the Burnt Bay boss!"

But the boys realized that kind of adventure could be dangerous to dogs and men, so they never hunted the champion of Burnt Bay again.

Nine

Of all Archie's boyhood jobs, perhaps that of "bird-minding" made the most lasting impression. During his young life almost all of the vast delta was planted in rice. It was the great Santee River flowing from the mountains of North Carolina and the fresh tidewater in this river that permitted plantation owners to grow rice here.

Some sixteen miles above the mouth of the Santee, the river divides into two great streams flowing parallel to the coast. At the time of Archie's youth, the Santee delta of more than a thousand acres had formed between these two rivers. The tide extended twenty miles upriver, rising about three feet at Hampton, which was seven miles from the ocean.

The entire delta was ditched and banked into various fields for planting rice. As long as Archie could remember he had watched the preparation of these fields. While the land was dry, rice was sowed. Then through an intricate system of dikes and floodgates, the Negro workers allowed the field to be covered with water to a depth of ten inches.

A romance developed around the growing of rice. Floodgates were named - Big Tom, Ajax, Old Man; so were the fields - Princess, White Oak, Carolina, and Rice Hope. Only during rice season did the Negroes sing certain songs. Taking great pride in their work, some of the workers became experts at various tasks. Among these were the workers who tended the canal heads or "trunks" that controlled the depth of the water in the fields. The pressure of fresh water from the rivers was so strong that the salt water tides did not intrude into the rice fields. Thus rice was planted all the way to the ocean. The grains would sprout beneath the water and grow up through it.

At intervals during this delicate process it was Archie's job to sit on the banks or dikes that divided the fields and "bird-mind."

In August when the grain became "in the milk," as the early stage was called, a constant watch was necessary to shoo away flocks of little yellow birds that descended upon their favorite food.

From the dikes Archie could look across the golden fields with their winding creeks and lonely reedbanks. It was here that he observed the haunting mystery of the tidewater land.

The most persistent intruder, the bobolink, sometimes called reedbird or ricebird, arrived out of the North in great numbers. When their autumnal flight brought them South, the birds arrived hungry and thin, but within a week they gorged themselves on their favorite food and became ridiculously fat.

In fact, they were so plump that if one fell on hard ground after being shot, it has been said he would sometimes burst open.

The individual flocks were usually not large, but when various flocks gathered at a rice field, the great numbers of them literally darkened the sky.

The minders employed all kinds of devices to keep these birds off the rice: whooping, beating on pails, and cracking whips. Some minders stood on platforms out in the fields. The best method of scaring these birds away was to shoot flattened buckshot at them. The whistling sound of the shot frightened the birds, and thousands could be roused from their eating this way. The Colonel claimed the buckshot was so effective because it sounded like the whirring of a great hawk's wings swooping over its prey.

Sometimes Archie would climb down from his station and creep through the rice to scare away the birds. This was dangerous business as his bare feet were susceptible to rattlesnakes and cottonmouth moccasins lurking there.

Working toward the feeding hosts, he passed among a few plump, yellow stragglers that he could almost catch with his hand. But keeping very still, he could hear the brilliant and jaunty males "bubbling of liquid glee," and shirring their bills as they husked the rice grains. Then he would fire his gun and wait for the great throngs of thousands to roar like thunder in sudden flight around him.

Once Archie stalked a small flock through a rice field flooded with water almost as deep as he was tall. Suddenly he came to an obstruction. Thinking it a big log floating in the water, he pushed it aside. When it did not float like a log, he realized it was a bull alligator about twelve feet long.

At night, birds would settle in the river marshes nearby; in the mornings the whole sky came alive with them. Sometimes they seemed to be a moving sky.

Once the rice was gathered, Archie's stint at bird minding ended for another year. This was the time, however, he liked to watch the birds flock to the fields and glean the rice dropped during reaping.

Archie particularly enjoyed the reaping of the rice. He liked to mingle with the Negroes as they cut rice with old-fashioned sickles. There was Isaac, the plantation sage, with his powerful muscles, and women like Paris, London, and Lisbon, with touches of color in their dresses or kerchiefs. Often they sang in beautiful rhythm as they worked. The Negroes could toil under heat that brought down the white man. Also, mosquitoes did not seem to bother them.

Unfortunately the ripened rice attracted mice and rats out of the woods, and these in turn attracted snakes. It was a common sight for a crowd of workers to cry out and scatter. The scene always meant **snake.**

One of the workers, Julia, was different from all the others. She would not run. Instead, she would approach the snake and, with a skillful sweep of her short-handled scythe, cut off his head. The Colonel often remarked that the workers would stop working until Julia came.

One afternoon as Archie sat on a narrow bank between rice fields to watch the reapers, he heard a low rumbling and looked up to see a huge black bull headed straight toward him. The monstrous animal paused now and then to paw at the ground with his front hoofs and to bellow before moving closer.

Archie looked around him. On one side lay a broad river - far too wide to swim even if it were not alive with alligators; on the other side of the dike ran a deep canal with a wild tangle of blackberry canes along the edges.

The great bull edged closer, swinging his head low to the ground his flared nostrils sweeping the grass on either side of him.

Two fields away Archie could see his father.

Suddenly the approaching bull gave a wild, weird bellow and reared back on his hind legs. His whole body writhed in pain. Archie watched in disbelief as he fell on the side of the bank, his flanks heaving.

As quickly as possible Archie cut a long heavy cane with the knife he always kept in his pocket. He was no longer afraid of the monster, for sounds coming from the grass told him what had happened. The great bull had been struck by a poisonous snake, no doubt deep into his nostril.

Bringing down the cane again and again, Archie thrashed the diamondback rattler on the edge of the dike.

Meanwhile the reapers had signaled the Colonel.

When his father reached him, the monstrous bull and the rattlesnake lay dead. The Colonel lifted his young son in his arms.

"Benjamin," he said, using the biblical name he gave his son when he wanted to show great love, "you must be more careful."

But even as his father spoke, it was obvious he doubted his words would influence his son to be less restless and adventurous. Still, being called **Benjamin** always gave Archie a special thrill.

Every day thereafter found Archie in the bright sunshine among the fragrant rice straw. He watched the heavy-headed rice lifted in golden sheaves from the stacks and spread out on the hard clay to be threshed.

Then the beating thud of the flails began. The joyous cries of Little One, Neuralgia, and other Negro children filled the air as they chased one another about the stacks while their mothers worked.

Since the rice sheaves were stacked in long rows in the barnyard, the visiting birds had access to the top layers. For the most part this plundering was allowed, for the weather was getting cold and the birds were hungry. Anyway, it was time for the feathered creatures to head southward.

At this time Archie studied redwings, grackles, and rusty blackbirds as well as cardinals, song sparrows, fox sparrows, whitethroats and an occasional bluejay, brown thrasher or towhee. Sometimes a cedar waxwing, mockingbird and various woodpeckers came to see what all the gathering was about.

Even the wild ducks knew when it was time to look for rice. At twilight they came from offshore sandbars and salt creeks and ponds near the coast. Along the delta they plunged their heads into the shallow water in search for spilled grain. Since they arrived after harvest time, they were no threat to the crop. Actually, they helped the rice planter by eating the leftover seed that might come up as a weak volunteer another season.

During the rice harvesting three- and four-masted vessels would tie up on the river behind Hampton to take rice to some distant port. Sometimes the ship would have to lie offshore until it got an east wind and a strong floodtide. Along with the fascination of it all, it seemed odd to Archie to see a sailing vessel in the woods.

This was an especially happy time of life for Archie. At night he would lie in bed and think of the mysterious ships docked nearby.

Ten

In 1730 when Hampton was built, the ballroom with its high vaulted ceiling and its intricately carved wainscoting was the setting of many gala affairs.

In Archie's time, however, it had other uses. At Christmas the little Negro children of the plantation would gather before a roaring fire in the cavernous fireplace to receive their presents. Besides gifts from the Rutledges, some presents were sent from northern friends who had visited Hampton. The younger children, dressed in Sunday clothes for the occasion, were led by the older ones who recalled earlier Christmases. Two long tables held toys, trinkets, candy, and clothing. In their joy and appreciation the children would begin to dance about the ballroom

On rainy days the Rutledge children romped and played in the ballroom. One summer Colonel Rutledge, for lack of a better place, had tobacco packed in the long room until the fragrant leaves could be shipped.

Many of the ballroom uses seemed a far cry from the silks and brocades of the courtly dancers of colonial days, who moved around the great room to the strains of a minuet. Still, the day the ballroom was turned over to the birds was the most unusual of all.

Unfortunately, in early December Tom had been wounded while hunting with a Charleston friend who had limited knowledge of guns. Since the shot was at fairly close range, Tom's life was in danger.

While he was recuperating, the doctor forbade him to leave the house. This was torture for Tom who, like Archie, loved the outdoors. Thus, Prince and Archie were kept busy trying to think of ways to amuse him.

Telling Tom of what they had seen in their trips to the woods and fields did not serve to entertain him but made him all the more restless and unhappy for not being there himself.

One December morning during this restless time Archie awoke to find the ground covered with snow and ice. Snow was rare in the South, and on the few occasions Archie had seen snow, it had been carried away shortly by a warm rain. But this snow had come to stay. The branches of trees leaned under their burden of ice and creaked under wind bearing down from the north.

As soon as Archie could pull on his clothes, he hurried to the back porch where Prince was waiting.

"De main field's full of ducks," Prince grinned. "An' I see four woodcock by de plum thicket. I mos' catch one."

Archie's excitement mounted. As he turned quickly to go back for his gun, he bumped into the Colonel on his way out of the house.

"Where to, Son?" his father asked.

Excitedly Archie told him what Prince had said about the ducks and woodcocks.

"I don't suppose the ducks mind the cold too much," his father remarked, "but I wouldn't shoot the woodcocks or any other birds. They are too numbed by the cold to show you a clean pair of wings.''

As much as the boys hated to admit it, they understood what the Colonel meant.

Prince, hating to see Archie's disappointment, spoke up: ''Mas' Henry's good to little buds like dey were chillun.''

Giving up the idea of getting his gun, Archie followed Prince out into the yard. ''But, Prince,'' he asked, ''how are we going to have any fun now?''

Prince shuffled his feet and said, ''Les go ketch dem woodcock to show Mas' Tom.''

Although it seemed doubtful to Archie that they would be able to catch wild fowl, he headed with Prince to the thicket of wild plum bushes.

Just as Prince had promised, there sat a beautiful black and rust-colored woodcock. His head and nail-like bill were drawn back against his body, and his round, wide-spaced eyes stared without blinking.

Archie had never been that close to a live woodcock before; and as he approached, the bird fluttered as though half-dazed, flared his wet tail feathers, and tried to fly.

Reaching out, Archie seized him and thrust him inside his warm hunting coat.

In a moment Prince and Archie had four more woodcocks, several robins, a cedar waxwing, and two song sparrows.

Triumphant, they headed back toward the house. Tom saw them coming and met them at the door. He could hardly believe his eyes, and it did Prince and Archie good to see him so happy.

As for Mrs. Rutledge, she was so pleased to see Tom happy that she gave her consent for the boys to keep the birds in the ballroom until after the cold snap.

The boys built a roaring fire of lightwood and live oak in the huge fireplace lined with blue Delft tiles. As the room warmed, the birds thawed and began to hop about and peck at grains of rice Tom had scattered on the floor. The woodcocks did not hop; they walked with great dignity of carriage. Their rust and black and brown colors had regained their velvety sheen.

Before long, the room was so warm that a song sparrow flew to the window sill and began little trills of a song.

Tom decided the birds should have food to which they were accustomed, so he directed Prince and Archie to hitch up the ox Cain to the single cart and drive out to get holly berries or whatever else they could find.

With the cart wheels crunching in the snow, the boys gathered great branches laden with berries from tupelo and cassena trees. They also found bunches of mistletoe, smilax, and red and black swamp-brier berries. On the way back they could not resist a big holly burdened with berries, so they cut the tree down and loaded it onto the cart.

Their hearts soared as they turned homeward with the cart laden with food for the wild birds.

By the gate a bird lay on the ground and a little farther several others huddled against the fence. Prince hopped down and scooped them up. One was a small southern yellow throat and the others fox sparrows with brown mottled coats.

Feeling proud that they had rescued these birds caught by the unexpected cold, Archie and Prince transferred their little captives to Tom at the door while they dashed back to lug in the vines, boughs and holly tree.

They stood the holly tree in the corner of the ballroom and wound the swamp vines and smilax in great green loops between the windows. Archie tacked the tupelo limbs over the windows, and Prince decorated the long mantel with scarlet cassena boughs.

The ballroom birdhouse became so successful that Tom sent the younger boys out into the biting cold again and again to bring in more birds.

In the shrubbery between the house and river they captured a golden thrush that was trying feebly to pick some wild-orange berries. Later they picked up a yellow-throated warbler, a chickadee, and three wax-wings. In a clump of frozen pokeweed stalks near the smokehouse they caught two catbirds. Beyond the stable in the bottom field they rescued a dozen sparrows and a ruby-crowned kinglet.

After three happy days of watching the pets, while always being careful not to startle them with sudden movements, the boys opened windows to the now pleasant weather.

As the birds began to feel the currents of fresh air, they began to fly outside. Many perched near the window in a big live oak and preened their feathers. None of them dashed away wildly. Instead, they acted as if they actually appreciated being saved from the cold.

Prince and Archie beamed. Not only had they saved many birds from a frozen death, but they had brought the best of the woods and fields to Tom at a time when he needed it most.

Indeed, their hearts were filled with the spirit of Christmas.

Eleven

From the age of six, Archie had hunted every kind of woods animal and fowl. He had hunted ducks from a boat paddled through mazy creeks and canals of the rice fields. He had used decoys and done flight shooting. And he had hunted in early morning and late evening.

But one hunt during his boyhood could never be forgotten. In late November Archie was shooting doves in a cornfield when he saw a huge bird fly overhead and alight on a birch tree at the edge of the field. Archie followed the great bird from tree to tree and at last shot it from a cypress.

Rushing home with his prey, he showed it to his father.

"Why, Son," the Colonel said, "that's a wild pigeon."

Immediately Archie could see that the bird was not an oversized dove, as he had thought. Now that his attention had been called to it, he could tell that the beautiful feathers of its shoulders and neck and its long tail distinguished it as a wild pigeon. Archie was always

ashamed to admit that he had mistakingly killed one of
the last wild pigeons in America.

Almost every day during the summer when the family
stayed in McClellanville, Archie would travel with his
father in a buggy the fourteen miles from the seacoast
and back. On these trips through the wildwoods, the
Colonel shared his knowledge and love of nature with
his young son. Archie particularly liked studying the
tracks of deer, fox, and wildcats.

Sometimes they would go on hunting trips to Mur-
phy's Island to shoot ducks. It was here the Colonel
taught Archie to remain motionless for long periods.
"A good hunter," he would say, "has to 'outquiet' his
game."

During their many jaunts together, the Colonel's
respect for the personal feelings of others made a deep
impression on Archie. He saw what one of the Negroes
meant when he said, "De Boss, he got feelin'."

Once Archie saw his father ride into a bay thicket to
break a great cluster of red roses for his wife. Archie's
mother would always put one of the flowers in her hair.

He remembered, too, the time he had been given a
new saddle with covered stirrups. A short time before,
Archie had been attempting to deliver clothes about
three miles down the road to Rose Boykin, the washer-
woman. Sluefoot, the horse he was riding, was always
hard to mount. But when Archie tried to get into the
saddle with a bundle of clothes tied in a sheet, the
animal became frightened and reared up. Archie's foot
slipped through the open iron stirrup and he was
dragged about a hundred yards.

"Benjamin," his father had said, "you have more
guardian angels than anyone I know."

Then, without saying anything about his plans, the
Colonel had ridden into Charleston and brought back a

handsome new saddle with covered stirrups.

Another day Archie had overheard an adult in this family say that his father had given his own war medal to an old soldier who hadn't received one. The medal had meant so much to the man that he insisted on being buried with it.

Colonel Rutledge, a true Southern gentleman, was even kind to his horse; on a hot day he would walk beside the animal to give him a rest.

In spite of his serious, pensive side, the Colonel could be witty, and often hummed rollicking old English hunting songs.

Even though Archie's relationship with his father was extremely close, especially since the death of Hugh, he still thought his father had odd ideas about some things. By the fireplace in the living room stood an ebony Chippendale armchair. For as long as Archie could remember, the left arm of the chair had lain in the closet of that room.

When Archie asked his father about it, the Colonel had told him that Hampton had served as headquarters of General Francis Marion, the Swamp Fox of the American Revolution.

"After one of General Marion's exhausting forays," he told Archie, "he was asleep in that chair when the Redcoat Banastre Tarleton surprised him. In springing up, Marion broke the arm off his chair."

Momentarily forgetting the chair, Archie had asked, "Did Tarleton get him?"

"Oh, no," the Colonel smiled. "You see, General Marion ran through the secret passageway to the back of the house, jumped on his horse, swam the river, and escaped into the wilds of the Santee delta."

"Well," Archie had asked, "why don't you fix the chair?"

"Oh," his father had answered, "I always thought it would be sacrilegious to repair what General Marion had broken."

His father had gone on to tell him about the parish Bible and prayer book taken by Colonel Tarleton, and of the great oak in front of Hampton. According to the family, the tree was going to be moved because it did not grow directly in front of the house. But when George Washington visited Hampton Plantation in 1791, he asked that the tree, then quite small, not be moved. Afterwards it was called the Washington Oak.

Their conversation had led Archie to think more about the secret passageway. The stairway leading to the cellar had always held a fascination for him. He had been told that during the time of slavery food was brought from the outside kitchen and into the dining room by way of the cellar stairway. But close by those stairs and the ones leading to the second floor of Hampton was an area that had been boarded over. In fact, inside, it had been covered by wallpaper and there was no access to it. Because Archie wanted so much to explore it, his imagination went wild when he thought of this hollow space, which as far as he knew, ran all the way to the roof. It is no wonder that he managed to link it with the ghost Hampton was rumored to have.

Hampton was close to the King's Highway. Since distances between plantations were great and travel of the day was slow, strangers journeying to Charleston at times were caught by darkness near their home. Thus, the Rutledges often boarded travelers overnight - everybody from whiskey drummers to bishops.

Once, just at twilight, an itinerant minister and his wife were unable to cross the Santee River because the ferry attendant was not on duty.

Mrs. Rutledge always had rooms for such travelers so

she was prepared when the couple sought lodging at Hampton for the night.

Winter evenings were long with Tom away at school, so Archie was glad to see new faces. It was always his duty to light the fire in the guest room. This was no great task as splintered lightwoood had been placed beneath the laid fire. It flared into flame at the touch of a match.

After supper the family and guests sat around the dining room fire talking. In the room overhead where earlier the guests had placed their black suitcase, a mysterious rocking began. Everyone heard it.

Now Hampton had been long known for its ghost. The odd raps, dragging sounds, and creepy noises had been explored through the years with lanterns, pokers, and guns, but no explanation had ever been found. Because the ghost only made noises and had never harmed anyone, the family had come to accept the strange occurrences.

Archie noticed the preacher begin to fidget in his chair. "A maid," he said, "must to preparing our room."

Immediately Mrs. Rutledge began making signs to Archie to keep quiet, but she was too late. "Oh," he blurted out, "that's just our ghost."

"Your what?" asked the minister.

Archie's parents tried to fake a laugh, and Archie felt all eyes upon him. Yet he could not keep quiet.

"If you listen," he urged, "you can hear it drag a body across the floor."

"Is this true?" the visitor questioned. His large ears seemed to protrude even farther and his eyes grew round.

Annoyed with Archie's persistence, the Rutledges tried to assure the man and his frail wife that they would indeed have a quiet evening.

In spite of the comforting remarks, they seemed edgy as Archie walked with them to their room to check on the fire.

"Son," the man asked, "isn't there another room we could sleep in?"

"Oh, you'll be all right," Archie said, "This was my great-grandmother's bedroom, and her ghost never bothers anybody."

Archie noticed the man shaking his head as he moved about peering into corners only dimly lighted by the flickering lamp and the firelight. Then he crossed to the bed where his suitcase lay open.

Suddenly the man let out a shriek and dashed wildly for the door.

"What is it?" The voice of the stern little woman echoed her fright.

In a second Archie was by the suitcase. "Why, it's only Ringwood. That old hound is always sleeping on the bed. Guess he liked your suitcase better."

"Little boy," the weasel of a woman said, "you live in a very strange house." She fixed her beady eyes on Ringwood, now slinking from the room.

Seeing her ill feeling toward their old pet hound, Archie attempted to make her more sympathetic. "He has mange," he offered.

As soon as the minister discovered the harmless source of his alarm, he reappeared.

While being scolded by his wife for running out and leaving her behind, he went once again to the suitcase on the bed. This time with shaking hands he lifted a flat-sided bottle to his lips and took a long drink.

Remembering that night was always great fun for Archie.

Twelve

Through his responsibilities as well as through his personal pursuits, Archie had many opportunities to observe coastal Carolina at night.

One such opportunity came when he was taking his turn as watchman over the tobacco shed.

Experimenting with tobacco as a crop, the Colonel had erected a shed for curing the tobacco at the intersection of several fields.

Because the temperature in the shed had to be kept constant and the bundles of leaves shifted periodically. someone had to be on guard day and night for about three weeks.

During Archie's six-hour watch, it was his job to open or close the windows to regulate the temperature and to expose different layers of the tobacco to the air to prevent molding.

On August nights when the moon was full, Archie would make his rounds of the racks of tobacco. Then he would sit in one of the low windows of the drying house and look out over the moonlit field. Here and there stood majestic live oaks.

Sometimes a deer ventured out into the pea field to feed. Archie watched the soft glow of the moon catch his shadowy profile at different angles. He appeared black and then silver, and at times he became invisible. Archie always marveled at the way the most silent of nature's creatures could be camouflaged by nature itself.

One night he watched a doe lead her two young fawns out into the moonlit field.

At first she looked, listened, and turned. Then she uttered a motherly sound understood by her young. With tender bleating the two fawns began to frolic, prancing and darting around their serene mother.

During the day they had stayed in a grassy bed, but in the safer hours of darkness they became fairies in the moonlight.

Building on such experiences, Archie was later to write that it was darkness that showed him the mighty trinity of existence - life, love, and death.

Another venture that offered Archie experience at night as well as by day was his work as a commercial fisherman. As a night fisherman he gained knowledge of dwellers of marshes and beaches. Sometimes sounds of battle broke the silence of the night. Wildcats often attacked raccoons living in the marshes.

One morning Archie found remains of a dead wildcat against a heap of dry sedge. Although the wildcat usually won in battle, this one had been drowned by a raccoon.

Other predators of the marshes included mice, which destroyed the nests of the little marsh hens.

Between the village of McClellanville and the ocean lay miles of salt marshes, creeks, and bays. Eastward lay Cape Romain, Cape Island, Raccoon Keys, and Sandy Point.

Before long Archie had learned the names of all the famous fishing spots along the salt sea marshes - Eagle Hummock, Oyster Bay, Five Fathoms Creek. He had learned, too, that the dunes and inlets with their long sandy beaches sometimes had a dangerous undertow.

In McClellanville Archie did not have his usual companion, Prince. Occasionally he fished with brother Tom. The two boys got to know many of the people of the village through their work as fishermen, and especially enjoyed a crippled man who always sat in his yard making oars of white ash. Sometimes he would be almost buried by huge piles of snowy shavings cut in making oars.

On good days Archie would catch at least a hundred fish. He sold them on a string of twelve fish for twenty-five cents. Of all his regular customers Archie enjoyed one man particularly. He was a large fellow, weighing over three hundred pounds, who always bought one string of fish for himself and one for his family. Sometimes Archie also had shrimp and crab for sale.

Once Tom and Archie were returning from fishing for bass along the marshes when they ran into a big school of mullet near the mouth of Tiger Creek, a deep estuary winding into the marsh fields.

They knew they could do nothing about the mullet then as these fish can rarely be caught with a hook and line, or for that matter, be caught in daylight.

Immediately they began to lay plans to catch mullet by blocking off the mouth of a small creek in the salt marshes with a gill seine. That way they could catch two or three dozen fish on a tide. Their only problem was that the high water they would need did not come in until midnight.

The two brothers left the wharf at eleven o'clock in order to row to the mouth of the creek, drive the stakes down, and stretch the net across before high tide.

Tom rowed their ten-foot cypress bateau, and Archie directed their course by watching the shoreline he knew by heart. The unusually heavy degree of phosphorus in the water made it possible for them to see, and the night lay still and warm under a starry sky.

A pull of half an hour down the channel brought them to Tiger Creek. For a while they sat on the rising water and listened to its telltale thudding, a sure sign of mullet.

They felt good. Just as they had planned, the fish were swimming into Tiger Creek.

When it was evident the school of mullet had gone into the creek, Tom rowed to the side so Archie could stake one end of the seine.

Carefully they stretched the net across to the opposite shore. Unfortunately, the net fell a little short of the width of the creek, so Tom staked the boat at the short end to try to help block off the opening.

Since Tom was older, he made the decisions when he was along, so Archie was surprised when he said, "All right, Arch, if you think you can keep the big ones from getting away, I'll run them down and you can tend the net."

Archie filled with pride as he saw his older brother splash off through the marsh with an oar over his shoulder to run the fish downstream toward the net.

Making sure the boat was secure, Archie slipped over the side and let himself down into the warm, sparkling water. Slowly he felt his way along the seine to make sure the corks were floating right side up and the lead line was set true.

The water was not as deep as he had thought and came slightly over his waist, but the bottom was soft and gooey. Several times he had to hold onto the seine to pull his feet out of the mud.

Before long Tom began to shout and Archie could hear him spanking the water near the head of the creek.

The water murmured; mullet jumped; and a big fish struck the seine and gilled himself.

The corks bobbed and the water foamed. Fish bumped against Archie's legs. Moving as fast as he could in water that had now risen to his chest, Archie grabbed at the trapped mullet and threw them into the boat. Again and again he seized the slippery fish and tossed them into the boat. Tom would be proud that he was getting so many, and big ones, too.

Suddenly a great frothing and churning of water near him caught Archie's attention. Up the creek Tom was still shouting and pounding with the oar, but whatever it was that was bumping against the seine was frightening the fish more than he or the net had.

By now his feet had bogged so far down in the sucking mud that he had to pull and lift the net to get to the gilled fish.

He was holding up a section of the wide net when a big wave lifted the water to his shoulder. **At that moment he saw the fin of a great shark move sluggishly downstream.**

Archie had heard that when a shark begins to circle on the surface that he is looking for trouble.

The thought of the son of the Cape Romain lighthouse keeper flashed through his mind. The boy had been killed by a shark, and Archie remembered the stoic faces of the group searching for what was left of his body.

His one thought was to get out of the water as quickly as possible. He tugged on the net to help pull his feet from the heavy mud, but as he did this he felt the stake pulling loose from the shore.

Tom was no longer shouting and beating. That meant he was heading back to join the sport of gathering the mullet. Archie could hear him tramping through the marsh, but he was still a long way off. His knees ached with strain; the tide and his sinking into the mud had brought the water up to his neck.

Not ten feet away he could see the shark. It had stopped by the boat. With all the voice he could muster Archie shouted for Tom. His brother answered. Yet Archie knew Tom was having a struggle of his own trying to cross a boggy inlet that the tide had filled, and that he could never reach him in time to help.

When the big creature turned away from the boat and headed toward him, Archie lost his head. He beat the water with his hands and screamed wildly "Shark! Shark!"

Catching the seine, Archie lifted it as high as he could and dropped it between him and the shark. Even the strongest of nets would have been no defense against such a creature, but for a moment the web baffled him and once again the shadowy form began to circle.

Then Archie saw the monster coming straight toward him. His fin rising above the water, he looked as if he summoned all the savagery in his great bulk for the final rush.

With the flow of the water the boat had loosed its moorings and swung upcreek at an angle. The next thing Archie knew, Tom had leaped into the boat and was shoving toward him. With his strong arms he pulled Archie up beside him.

The tall knife-fin of the tiger shark flashed by the stern of the boat and tore through the net as if it had been a cobweb.

The boat trip home helped to calm the brothers, and when they got to the village that night, they stretched their net between two pines to dry. The next morning they saw where the shark had gashed the net. The tear measured two feet across and three feet vertically, enlarged by the dorsal fin on the huge fish.

Although Archie endured previous encounters with a sting ray and even an octopus, he often said this experience with the shark was the most frightening.

As far as he was ever able to determine, this was one of the largest sharks ever to be seen in local waters.

His father had to be right - a guardian angel was watching over him that night in Tiger Creek.

Thirteen

About five miles downriver from Hampton and two miles from the ocean lay a strange, sandy plateau called Tranquility. It stood twelve feet above the level of the marsh grasses and rice fields. The Rutledges owned a little hunting shack on this mound, and it became a favorite place for Archie to go duck hunting. As a young boy he loved to go with his father through the winding creeks where wild ducks abounded in such numbers they blackened the sky.

Sometimes they did flight shooting; other times they used decoys.

When Archie was older, he often left home in the afternoon on the high ebb tide and rowed the three-hour trip down to Tranquility alone. All along the way he flushed out ducks that would swim out of the edges of the marsh just ahead of his canoe. Even so, he did not shoot. He knew his destination was a paradise for wild duck and shore birds and there would be no trouble getting all he needed once he reached Tranquility. Besides, he had only twenty-five shells, and he wanted to make the most of each shot.

The only inhabitants of the small island were London Legare and his wife Sarah. When Archie would go down to hunt, they would take care of him.

One November after greeting the couple at sundown, Archie walked to the southern edge of the hill that sloped away to the marsh. There he crouched behind a clump of bushes. The rush of wings and the moving cries of birds made him feel that the whole world belonged to wildlife and he was an intruder into their beautiful domain. Always on the evening of his arrival he was far too fascinated with his surroundings to think about shooting.

When the sun went down and he returned to the Legares, Sarah served him a meal of black bass, rice, sweet potatoes, wild duck, and coffee.

Archie was always in his heaven there. The affection was warm between him and the couple whose parents had been slaves of Archie's ancestors, and they always talked long into the night.

Once in bed Archie felt he would fall right to sleep, but it was always the same. The clamor of thousands of wild ducks kept him awake most of the night. Occasionally there would be a period of silence; then once again thousands of birds complained to the night sky.

The next morning at daybreak London called him to a breakfast of hominy, pork chops, corncakes, and coffee.

Afterward London would paddle Archie through Atkinson's Creek and other meandering canals and ditches of the delta. London, an expert oarsman, never let his dripping cypress blade touch the boat, and he rarely made a ripple in the water.

Besides giving Archie advice about shooting, London would, just as the Colonel did, show him signs of wildlife: a sandbar where a bald eagle had eaten a mallard, or where an otter had made a mud bank into a slide.

Taking London's advice to let a duck "get the jump out of his system" before shooting, Archie succeeded in bringing down a great number.

He was careful, however, to use his shells wisely and wait for good shots. Even with his single barrel gun, he would sometimes down with a single shot more than one of the dozen or more rising ducks.

When the tide was about half high, Archie would begin the long trip homeward. No matter how tired he was from the physical exertion of rowing so far, his adventure proved worthwhile.

The tidal marshes of Cape Romain became another of Archie's favorite places to hunt. Not far from the mouth of the Santee River, these marshes were meshed by creeks. Nearer the shoreline the soil changed from mud to sand, and open tidal flats had formed where the tide moved in and out. These sandy flats along the Atlantic seaboard harbored shore birds.

One fall morning when Archie was twelve, he went to the tidal flats to hunt. Under a pearl sky the air was crisp as he headed toward his "blind," a gnarled old cedar in the midst of a clump of sea grasses.

Archie particularly like to bring down the Spanish curlew or sicklebill. The big bird had long, slender legs and his great bill curved downward in a graceful arc. On the ground he carried himself with an elegant gracefulness; in flight he usually fell into a triangular formation with the others cruising above the shoreline on great cinnamon-lined wings. Their fluting calls lingered with Archie long after the hunt was over.

On this particular day as he waited for the curlews, he observed flocks of sanderlings, ruddy turnstones, sandpipers, black-bellied plover with their great yellow legs, and some Hunsonian curlews. Long lines of teal sped by on their way to favorite ponds on the barrier islands.

Just at sunrise a small flock of the long-billed curlews headed Archie's way. Coming in low and in their usual slow wing-beat flight, they made a perfect target. Archie shot, killing one bird and breaking the wing of another.

Much to his surprise, the wounded bird made no attempt to seek refuge in the marshy borders, but, even with his drooping wing, sauntered back and forth with the dignity so typical of his breed. As he did so, he called to his mates with a loud musical cry. His behavior made him a perfect decoy for Archie. The flock turned and came back, making it possible for him to take two more of the large birds.

Then for some reason he could not explain, Archie decided not to shoot any more. The bird's sad calling and the other birds' answering of the call, even at the risk of their own lives, touched him. The flock kept returning for their mate who could no longer fly, but Archie refused to shoot.

Instead, he watched the other birds. Near him ran a flock of plover with their curious way of running a little way, then stopping and repeating the maneuver. Archie liked to think of the ghostly little creatures as "fairies of the land."

When it was time for Archie to return home, he caught the curlew with the broken wing and carried it the seven miles to his home. Once there, he made a splint for its broken wing and fed it fiddler crabs. When the wing had healed, he took the bird down to the beach where he had wounded him and turned him loose. Once again the curlew called up his companions. They came in stately flight, and this time Archie's bird joined them.

Fourteen

When Archie became thirteen, his parents decided that he should enter Porter Academy in Charleston. Mrs. Rutledge had determined early in her son's life that he should be educated at any sacrifice. At Porter, too, discipline would be an integral part of his education.

In Charleston Archie boarded with a Dr. and Mrs. Baker, friends of his mother's. At first he suffered from terrible homesickness. He did not care for the regimentation of the school, and his stiff uniform only added to his discomfort.

Although discipline was strict, Archie spent much of his class time longing for the woods and fields of Hampton. He daydreamed in class, drawing pictures of himself rowing on the old South Santee River and shooting wild ducks on ponds. He even lined up the decoys in his sketches.

Occasionally he edged his paper with a wounded buck at bay or a dog pointing a partridge.

Daily Archie reminisced about the wildlife of the Santee that he knew so well. Often he thought of the

When Archie was thirteen years old, his parents sent him to Porter Military Academy in Charleston.

stag with the distinctive hoof print. The animal's right hoof was twisted so that its print was readily identified by local hunters. Archie knew of this male deer even when it was a fawn. He knew what paths he took in the dewy hours and where he loved to roam. Like the human spirit he always returned to the places he loved. Archie felt a strange kinship with this wild creature, for the lure of his own home was irresistible.

On the weekends that Archie did get home, he spent Saturday mornings hunting. He usually made a record of his "catch" inside his closet. One list read:

> 4 snipe
> 5 doves
> 6 quail
> a rabbit
> a squirrel
> a hawk

Once his homesickness began to wear off, however, Archie found his teachers kind and inspiring. Perhaps his Latin teacher made the most lasting impression. A colorful character, the teacher chewed tobacco and kept a spittoon on his desk. A strict disciplinarian, he was known to send boys home for mocking him. Yet Archie met his favor and beamed with pride when the teacher returned a paper to him with the comment: "As solid as a stone wall in Georgia."

Since some French had been spoken at Hampton in the presence of servants and children, Archie already had some knowledge of that language as well as of Latin, Spanish, and Greek. Thus, he excelled in languages. At the Academy he received medals in French and first prize in English.

His math teacher, however, would get exasperated with him over his lack of mathematical knowledge. In fact, Archie often felt his professor's disgust even

While at Porter, Archie received the medal for first prize in English in 1900. He also received medals in French.

though no comment was made. Later Archie was to learn that any time some student would "pull a boner" in that teacher's class, he would dash down an eraser and exclaim, "You'll never amount to a thing. You are just like Archibald Rutledge!"

One Christmas holiday while Archie was at the academy, the headmaster decided on the spur of the moment to dismiss the students a day early. The Colonel had already made plans to meet his son in a horse and buggy the following day, and Archie had no way of notifying him otherwise.

In spite of these plans, Archie could not stand the thought of giving up this extra day at Hampton. Thus he set out on foot, crossed the ferry to Mount Pleasant, and half ran all night long the fifty miles to Hampton. At daybreak he arrived, a tired but happy young man.

While Archie was a student at Porter, some of the verse he wrote appeared in magazines and newspapers. The beauty and charm of life as well as its areas of gloom were having a lasting effect on Archie. Being a reader, he naturally wanted to write down his own feelings. Although his writing had never been taken seriously by members of his family, particularly an aunt who bitterly criticized his efforts, it was important to him. So much in earnest was he that at this age he drew up a Writer's Creed:

> I believe in God, in immortality, and in a region
>   where eternal spirits dwell.
> He who loves virtuous beauty is holding fast to
>   the hand of God.
> Human wealth, power, and cunning avail not
>   against cosmic justice.
> Be guided by your admirations, not by your disgusts.
> To praise another does you more good than him or her.
> All the laws of nature are on our side.
> Grief is life's challenge to us to be great.
> The heroes and heroines all about us are those
>   who refuse to linger where they have bled.
> Beauty and truth are the language of God; virtue
>   is the behavior of God; love is the will of God.
> The laws of nature are the hand of God on the
>   controls of the universe.
> To the reader, the writer owes a moral responsibility.

Now the Colonel was proud of his son's hunting ability and of his honors in school, but he was unsure of his feelings when it came to a son who wrote poetry.

When Archie's verse appeared in print, the Colonel would stick the newspaper under his coat and show it to the Presbyterian minister who lived up the street from them in McClellanville. Although Colonel Rutledge had great respect for the minister's opinion, he always returned home confused and dubious.

If Archie's father thought poetry made his son any less a man, he was mistaken. Once a Porter student who was delivering mail carelessly threw a letter from Archie's mother into a mud puddle. Archie fought with him and in the tussle received a broken nose.

Going to Porter Academy had caused Archie pain in separating him from his homelife; leaving for Union College in New York at the age of sixteen was far worse.

Scholarships were available to promising students of need. As salutatorian at Porter Academy, Archibald received the honor of pursuing his education as a Lorillard Scholar.

When he and his mother looked at Schenectady, New York, on the map, it seemed a long, long distance away. There were no good roads at this time and no buses or cars for traveling. Just the thought of going such a distance made Archie so homesick that for weeks in advance family members began to doubt his ability to live so far from home.

When the time finally arrived, Archie stood at dusk on the front porch of Hampton listening to the music of wild ducks' wings passing overhead. In the distance he could hear the Negroes laughing and talking. The old hound Ringwood sidled up to him to be patted on his head.

A visiting uncle observed Archie's pensive mood. "I think," he said, "Archie will end up jumping in the creek."

Archie had no intention of jumping in the creek, but he did envy the Negroes and the others who could stay at Hampton. He thought of a school friend named Andrew who had become owner and captain of a sloop carrying freight to and from McClellanville, Charleston, and Georgetown. He envied the free and outdoor life that would be his.

All this Archie would be giving up for a confined academic life.

Thinking so seriously about it all, he even stopped shooting quail, deciding they were too beautiful to kill.

Now that his last days at home had become a reality, Archie racked his brain to think of something to take with him from home and finally came up with the idea of scuppernong wine.

Not only was he unsure of just how to make the wine, he was unaware of how difficult it would be to transport it.

Once he had made the wine, he buried two bottles of the "green" liquid in his new trunk under shirts and pajamas.

The night before he was to leave for school, a loud noise awakened the family. There was an explosion in the trunk.

The observant uncle who was sleeping downstairs jumped up and shouted, "I thought so! Archie has shot himself!"

Mrs. Rutledge forgave her son for the inconvenience he caused her in redoing his clothing, and the next morning Archie sailed on a sloop called the **Virginia Belle** to Charleston.

There he caught a liner for New York. A Pinckney cousin who saw him off from Charleston worried that he was going into "enemy territory."

At first Archie did feel like a lonely rebel, but he found his roommates J.H. Small and John Parker to be a great comfort.

"I promised to write every Sunday and Wednesday," he wrote home, "so here goes. I am getting on fine, but I miss everybody. It isn't exactly homesickness, but the thought that I don't know when I will see you all again - that's the only thing that worries me."

One of his first letters told of the asphalted streets, a

sight he was unaccustomed to. Always his letters were signed "Your loving son, Ar."

"I didn't know the Yankees could be so nice," he wrote another time. "I get invited out to some meals and the president has been nice to me."

He usually ate at a restaurant called Claphem's where he was known as "Johnny Reb." Someone told the owner Archie had a tough time financially, so about once a week he handed back Archie's lunch ticket without punching it.

To help with his schooling Archie took on odd jobs. He worked in gardens, shoveled snow, tended furnaces, corresponded for a chain of papers, and cleaned classrooms.

"I am very careful with money," he wrote home. "My meals are $3.75 a week. I find I can save some on my washing. You remember we thought it would be about $3.00 a month."

Although Archie filled most of his time with work and study, he ran track for Union. He high-jumped and ran the high and low hurdles and the mile. Once he wrote, "I went on a cross-country run yesterday, a two and one half mile run, but I got winded about 200 yards of the goal."

Archie wrote, too, about the climate. "It makes me feel fine," he said, "but I don't care if I never see snow again. You should see the Erie Canal. It was frozen over and is a pretty sight at night when it is lighted up and hundreds of people are on it at one time. Everything is a solid sheet of ice, and I am getting a few 'high falls' learning how to skate."

Occasionally he wrote about the lighter side of college. "Monday night a gang of sophs caught me and made me sing and dance. Then I had to mix paste with my hands and go out all over town and post bills. (I enclose one.) I got back here at 2:30 a.m. I didn't mind too much especially as a 'cop' got after me and I had a good deal of fun getting away.''

He told, too, about the cane rush - a sophomore-freshman scrap with not-too-fresh eggs, tomatoes, and salt: "The boys up here go together with fraternities. I am in with a very nice crowd in Kappa Alpha. They are all gentlemen.''

Archie found biology, physiology, algebra, French, and German extremely hard. "None of the studying I did at Porter Military can compare with that I have to do here," he wrote home. "I hope you understand why I am not continuing Latin. It was not because I didn't like it, but I could not help myself. I was twelve books behind.''

And there were always reminders that he missed Hampton and his family. "I had a pretty hard 'spell' of homesickness when your last letter came. Write often as you don't know how good it is to get your letters when you're 900(?) miles away. Tell Tom and Papa when they are counting how many turkeys they can get at a shot from the blind to think of me. But tell Papa that he must not write to me about the turkey blinds as it fills me with longing.''

Concerning food, he wrote, "I miss rice badly - have not had it but once and that was for dessert. But it is potatoes - morning, noon, and night.''

Always Archie mentioned the trees and shrubs in his letters. "Ask Aunt Mame if the grape vine I planted is living, and I hope the hemlocks are growing.''

He wrote, too, that he had taught his roommates "Roll Jordan" and "Reborn Again" so they could sing with him.

As all the other fellows, Archie had a "home corner" in his room, and he constantly asked his mother to send

While at Union College, Archie edited the college newspaper and was class poet.

him something else for his spot. He requested pictures of Hampton, rice, Spanish moss, and some partridge berries.

Late one evening after receiving a letter from home, Archie went for a walk down an old road near the campus. His father had just written to tell him of going to Sandy Point where he caught fish and found turtle eggs.

"If only I could go home for a visit," he thought as he sat on a stone wall near the campus. To his right the Mohawk River ran full and dark. Soon the sound of hoof beats and an old-fashioned buggy interrupted his reverie.

"Aren't you from Union?" a voice asked. "You look lonely."

To his surprise the conversation ended with an invitation to dinner in a beautiful home with silver and paintings. Not only did he find a friend, but the friendship led him to a job.

"I see prospects for a job," he wrote home the next day. "but it will mean that I won't get home even in the summer. I don't want you to worry though. I never stop thinking of what a burden I am to you. Sometimes I wish I had not come here but had gotten a job to help you along."

Before long Archie learned that being from the South and having a knowledge of wildlife would pay off. Charles Proteus Steinmetz, who had been exiled from Germany in his youth for expressing his views on sociology, was now considered the genius of General Electric. A frail, deformed man with an eccentric manner, he kept many unusual pets for companionship. As these included poisonous snakes and alligators, he had considerable trouble feeding them. On hearing from Archie's dinner host about a college student from the South who understood dangerous animals, Steinmetz sent for him.

Besides helping himself through college by feeding the great man's pets, Archie became closely associated with this man of genius and fame.

Almost every week the news carried a story about some achievement by Steinmetz. Yet if he was aware of all this publicity, he never gave a sign of it in Archie's presence. Once after blaring headlines claimed "Steinmetz Makes Lightning Strike," Archie called his attention to this article.

With deep-set, mystic eyes, he looked at Archie a moment, then said, "Archie, boy, we know nothing."

From this simple statement Archie came to realize that even great men can be humble.

Still another letter home asked, "If you send a box, try to put some 'game' in it so these Yankees will believe me when I tell them I come from God's country."

"I wrote my last essay on 'My Ole Southern Home,'" he said another time. "I tried to do old Hampton justice - right down to the ghost."

"I have stopped drinking tea and coffee and drink only milk now. I weigh 190 lbs. and am 6'4"."

Always thinking of his friends at Hampton, Archie hoped to send some of the outgrown clothes to Prince when he had a chance.

After mentioning in several letters what a temptation it was to smoke, Archie finally wrote, "I didn't know whether to tell you I was smoking or not. But, Mama, a fellow can't come out of college without it. It helps me to study."

When word got around that "Johnny Rebel" could do almost anything, Archie began to be called on for odd things. Once a cow was put on the third floor of the physics lab. How the person who played the joke got the cow there no one knew, but neither did anyone know how to get her back down. A teacher told Archie if he would bring her down, he would be excused from classes for the day.

Quick to make plans, Archie went to a nearby farm and got some corn and a rope from a farmer. Back in the lab he pled and urged the old bony animal down one step at a time.

When Archie finally made it to the bottom with the cow, a crowd had gathered to cheer his success.

On another occasion while he was working at a part-time job for General Electric, an employee developed smallpox, giving everyone a good scare. It was decided that all employees should take vaccinations against the disease. In some way the authorities heard that Archibald Rutledge had an interest in medicine. As a result, they drafted him to give immunizations to about five hundred female employees.

The girls decided that since they did not want the unsightly scars caused by the inoculation to be on their arms, they would have the vaccination just above the knee.

Now Archie had come to college with a thorough knowledge of French and English but with considerably less knowledge of the opposite sex. From his mother's example, he took for granted that all women were angels and treated them as such.

When he arrived at work the next morning, a long line of giggling girls waited for him. He spent most of the day in flushing embarrassment as he completed the immunizations on the girls' legs.

Archie did not, however, continue his interest in medicine. He was later to admit that he seemed to turn faint at the dissecting table.

Admitting to a weakness in mathematics, Archie wrote home: "I passed through mathematics in the dark. Sines, cosines, logarithms, and square roots gave me indigestion."

"Besides," he said, "physics do not tell how a star is hung, nor explain the retiring beauty of a fringed gentian but ignore the wild and wonderful spirit of man."

Always, though, Archie had a way with words. As a senior he won first prize in an oratorical contest. Oddly enough his speech dealt with secession, a doctrine which the majority of his audience and the judges did not approve.

He edited the college newspaper and he was class poet. Ever aware of his debt to his parents, he wrote a poem to his mother.

If mountains for me stood aside,
If seas a pathway through their tide
Made for my feet, if now I stand
Safe in a fair and radiant land,

Ah, not by me the deed was done!
Not by my strength was victory won!
My mother had a faith in me
To move the mountains and the sea.

I heard her voice behind me call
In love; she kept me 'gainst my fall;
I passed the wave, the gloomy wood,
Because her heart believed I could.

O trust divine, sustaining, true,
I, who achieved because of you,
Now take the garlands and the crown
At your dear feet to lay them down.

No matter where life would lead, memories of home and family would always be with him: the mockingbirds, Carolina wrens, the calling of the wild ducks, the wind in the pines, the voice of his mother reading, and the Negroes singing "Jesus Will Fix It for Me" and "Deep Down in My Heart."

Fifteen

In 1904 when Archibald was graduated as valedictorian from Union College, he tried a variety of jobs. He sold telephones in Washington, D.C., only to learn that he was no salesman. For a while he worked for Excelsior Water Filter Company, and later with a patent attorney.

His next job on **The Washington Post** proved to be a frustrating one. Just after joining the **Post,** Archibald covered a murder on the Potomac waterfront. He did such an outstanding job the editor wanted more of the same. Once he asked sharply, "What, Archibald, no murder today?"

"Well," Archibald threw back at him, "you did not expect me to commit one, did you?"

Even though the young reporter held his own with what he described as "garbage stories," he found after a few months of reporting that he was far more restless than he had ever been and that he was broke.

Now five months out of college and not yet twenty-one, he registered at a teachers' agency. As a result, he received a call to substitute for two weeks at Mercersburg Academy in Pennsylvania.

The train trip to take the temporary teaching job did anything but boost his already low morale. To begin with, the train was late. When it finally did arrive, it looked quite run-down. Worse still, its steam pressure was so low that every time the engineer blew his whistle, and he did so often and furiously, the train slowed. Once it stopped completely.

At a small way station called Marion, Archibald had to change and take a southbound train for Mercersburg. It was getting late and raining steadily when he got off to make the change, and there was no waiting room. To add to the dismal atmosphere, the train also carried a casket. As a matter of fact, the body, which he learned was a murder victim, and Archibald were the only passengers.

When the train finally did reach Mercersburg, a delegation met the casket, but no one from the Academy met Archibald.

That evening "The Hill," as Mercersburg Academy was called, was celebrating a football victory. Even before Archibald reached the campus, he could hear the uproar coming from its six hundred male students.

When Archibald finally found the headmaster's house, his wife came tripping down the stairs. Archibald thought she was a picture of beauty in her snowy dress with a broad blue sash.

He knew he must look rumpled, but he was not prepared for her skeptical look when he told her he had come to substitute teach. He was even less prepared for her words.

"Why," she laughed, as if the whole idea of his coming to Mercersburg were preposterous, "you'll never do. You are much too young."

"Your husband sent for me," Archibald heard himself reply.

As she ushered him into the living room where others chatted enthusiastically, Archibald had the feeling some tragic mistake had been made.

When the football team came clomping in, Archibald began to feel that she was right. Could he, a twenty-year-old "string bean," as he often called himself, teach these giants?

He was even more convinced when not a single member of the team offered to chat with him.

Later Archibald met Dr. William Irvine, the headmaster. In spite of his wife's earlier evaluation, Dr. Irvine hired Archibald for the job.

When after two weeks Archibald was employed for the rest of the year, he was humiliated to have to borrow his fare back to Washington to make arrangements for the move.

He had arrived in Mercersburg with only fifty cents in his pocket. He returned to Washington on Sunday to find that no trains were in operation. He had no choice but to walk the ten miles to Greencastle to catch a train in the Main Line.

Once settled at Mercersburg Academy, Archibald learned that this spot in the lower Cumberland Valley had been an important station on the Underground Railroad, which had helped slaves flee to the North during the Civil War. Being the son of a Confederate Colonel, he could not help feeling apprehensive about being in "enemy territory."

It bewildered and saddened him to think that some of the older men of Mercersburg had perhaps helped to devastate his beloved South. The name of "Johnny Reb" had followed him from college, but he wasn't at all sure that here it was meant affectionately.

Archibald found, however, that the old Union soldiers liked talking with him. One of them became such a loyal friend that at his death he left Archibald his entire library.

On the eve of Memorial Day as Archibald walked in a cemetery, he came upon the graves of soldiers that had been remembered with flowers and little American flags. To his surprise the graves of three Confederates had been honored, too.

He was so touched by this lack of prejudice that he wrote an article about it for the **Times-Dispatch** of Richmond, Virginia.

A few days later he received a letter from an elderly woman who said that when she was a young bride her husband was reported "missing in action" during the war. She believed this might be her husband's grave and asked if she might come to Mercersburg to view it.

On the day of her arrival a northern band played "Dixie," and old Union soldiers covered their hearts with their caps.

From that time on Archibald knew that he was no longer in an alien land. He knew, too, that he no longer wanted to be just a Southerner but an American.

As it turned out, Archibald stayed at Mercersburg Academy thirty-three years.

The grounds of the school covered 120 acres, but the surrounding country with its fields, woods, and clear rippling streams was free to the boys of the school. Archibald won the hearts of his students by sharing his love of nature. Together they spent long hours hunting arrowheads in the fields nearby.

Later he recorded much of his philosophy of teaching in a book entitled **When Boys Go Off to School,** published by Fleming H. Revell Company, an international publisher.

"As for purposes of instruction," he wrote, "courtesy is a far more penetrant lance than sarcasm;

and it leaves no wound to be forgotten - or remembered."

"Tolerance, patience, kindliness," he also said "- these are worth infinitely more than venom and violence."

He wrote further that "The teacher's fight is with the subjective foes; with everything that is wrong in thought, reasoning, feeling, motive."

Typical of Archibald's own upbringing, the school stressed strong character. After dishonor, the worst trait was snobbery, for here the boy who earned his way studied by the boy whose family had great wealth. President Calvin Coolidge's sons were among these boys.

"Without work," the school's motto ran, "man can be given credit for little; without faithful effort he is neither of economic nor spiritual value to himself or anyone else."

The Academy allowed no room for laziness. If a boy's average fell below passing, he was put in study hall for two weeks. If after that time he had not pulled up his average, he retained a seat there. All mornings with vacant periods, and each evening, were spent in the study hall.

An infraction of a rule brought on hours of guard duty carrying heavy weapons. Until the imposed discipline had been met by being walked off at the rate of one hour a day, no vacations were allowed.

Strong in the support of missions, the Academy believed in hard work, fair play, and a clean life.

Nearly every week some famous persons would come to speak to the students, and the headmaster and his wife were quite generous about having Archibald meet them, mostly writers.

Among these visitors was Jack London of whom Archibald said, "He talked tough and tried his best to look like a wilderness lout, which he certainly was not."

The editors of **Outlook** and **Outdoor Life** came, and Dr. Charles Eraman, the president of the Theological Seminary at Princeton. It was he who suggested to Archibald that he do some inspirational writings.

Although Archibald's love of writing was enhanced by all of the famous authors who visited the Academy, perhaps the one who impressed him most was Henry Van Dyke of Princeton. Already famous himself in literary circles, he took a sincere interest in the young South Carolina English teacher and gave him much encouragement in his writing.

Dr. Van Dyke came to the school each spring and stayed a week. He preached on Sunday and spent the rest of the time trout fishing. Archibald was delegated as his guide for this sport.

Of course this pleased Archibald, who always enjoyed the woods of nearby Cumberland Mountain. He particularly liked turkey hunting in the Valley. Having made the acquaintance of "a real turkey hunter" named Seth, Archibald hunted with him in the wilds of Path Valley, Bear Valley, on Sidelong Hill, in the Big Cove, and on Two-Top Mountain.

Knowing of his love of hunting, his students gave him a Parker shotgun. Thus, Archibald took refuge from his busy academic life in the Tuscorora hills. Not far away a freight train on the B & O might be shrieking for a crossing, making the air tingle with sound. But in the woods the air breathed of hemlock, wild grapes, and pine, reviving his chronic nostalgia for the fields and streams of Hampton.

Sixteen

Dr. William Mann Irvine, the headmaster of Mercersburg and an inspiring leader, became like an older brother to Archibald. Mrs. Irvine took a great deal of teasing over her initial greeting to him. This was especially true after her sister Florence visited in Mercersburg and Archibald fell in love with her.

Florence Louise Hart was born in Memphis, Tennessee, where her father, Major Camillus Sluman Hart, was a Mississippi steamboat captain. "Floy," as she was called, was often spoken of as one of the "Four beautiful Hart sisters." A poet in her own right, she shared Archibald's love of writing.

In December of 1907 when Floy was living in Winchester, Virginia, and working in the Treasury Department, she and Archibald were married.

The school reconditioned a farmhouse for them, and they called their new home Woodland, as a reminder of Hampton.

When in 1908 a son, Archibald, Jr., was born, Archibald learned that persistence was a real virtue. He was beginning to receive national acclaim for his

*Archibald Rutledge married Florence
Hart, sister of the wife of the headmaster
at Mercersburg Academy.*

writing, and now after a day in the classroom he wrote
long into the night. Soon his first book of verse, **Under
the Pines,** was published.

He wrote articles about birds and other wildlife for
the **Virginia Quarterly** and **The Georgia Review.** The
University of Georgia published a book of his poetry
under the title of **The Everlasting Light.**

During this time Archibald did some public speaking,
chiefly at clubs, churches, schools, and colleges. At first
he spoke only in Pennsylvania, Maryland, and Virginia,
but soon he was called to St. Louis, Atlanta, and
Chicago.

Everywhere he found people kind and gracious. He
learned early that the best way to get an audience and
keep it was to humanize what he had to say.

For many years he had through his love of turkey hunting experimented with a wild turkey call which he christened "Miss Seduction" because it sounded like a love call. It was a small box with the ends and bottom of white pine, the sides of basswood, and the cover of black locust - one of the hardest woods.

Often Archibald would take his turkey call to the speaker's platform to begin a lecture on Shakespeare by demonstrating its enticing lure. His audiences always responded enthusiastically.

Being fond of all facets of nature and being a practical gardener, he also wrote for many farm and gardening magazines.

After the birth of Henry Middleton IV in 1910 and Irvine Hart in 1912, Archibald was even more aware of the need to receive money for his writing. One company published his books **Day Off in Dixie** and **Children of the Swamp and Wood;** another put out **Wild Life of the South, Old Plantation Days, Tom and I on the Old Plantation,** and **An American Hunter.** Some of these dealt with Low Country lifestyle, especially during his childhood; others with the wildlife of the Low Country and with his life of hunting.

Later another company began to publish small books made from Archibald's inspirational articles which had first been printed in magazines. **The Meaning of Love, The Flower of Hope, The Angel Standing,** and **A Wildwood Tale** were among these little volumes.

Proclaiming that Rutledge's messages came through to them, readers everywhere took him to their hearts. When his book **Peace in the Heart** described peace as "the inner fulfillment of one's own personality through appreciation of God's world," he reached the very soul of his reader.

Sometimes Archibald would have to escape his busy

home and take refuge in an empty classroom in order to write.

Fortunately, Floy shared her husband's love of writing and understood his desire to express his feelings in words. In 1911 she published her own book of verse under the pen name of Dixie Wolcott, taking her pseudonym from a distant relative, Oliver Wolcott, a signer of the Declaration of Independence.

In spite of his busy working schedule, Archibald found time to be with his young sons. Just as the Colonel had taken him to the fields of Hampton, he took his boys to the countryside. After frost had killed the summer greenery, they hunted in the wheat stubble of southern Pennsylvania. Along fence rows where briars and bushes grew and in the thickets and woodlots they flushed out coveys of quail.

In summer they planted a garden together and the boys sold fruit, especially strawberries. Archibald bought a goat and harnessed him to a wagon for his young sons' business venture.

Although Floy was skeptical, she saw the excitement of her sons and went along with the idea. She always saw to it that the three were dressed in identical white sailor suits and caps when they started out to sell their berries. Only one slight problem developed: Irvine, the youngest boy, insisted on eating the big strawberries off the tops of the baskets.

The vegetable cart proved so successful that when the garden was depleted, the boys and their father picked wild berries from the fields and along the streams for the boys' wagon.

Archibald felt that his sons' four-year business venture not only afforded the family an opportunity to save money for the boys' education but it taught them the value of money.

About now Archibald's book **Hunter's Choice** was published. He was also writing articles for **The Saturday Evening Post** and **Reader's Digest.**

Money was scarce during these years and the sale of articles to magazines such as **Good Housekeeping, American Magazine,** and **Field and Stream** was important to the Rutledge family. Winning a short story contest in **Outdoor Life** brought much satisfaction as well as $800.

In June of 1921 the Colonel died at the age of eighty-three. Since Archibald had come to New York to attend Union College, he had returned to Hampton only on visits. Each year his family spent Christmas there, and the Rutledge boys always looked forward to being with their grandfather, "Colonel Daddy."

Upon the death of her husband, Mrs. Rutledge left Hampton to live with her daughters, Caroline and Mary.

Four years later Mrs. Rutledge died. She was buried alongside her husband and son Hugh at St. John-in-the-Wilderness Cemetery in Flat Rock, North Carolina.

Money was scarce and times were getting even harder. Archibald continued to write. He expanded one of the chapters from his book **Peace in the Heart** to make a little book called **Life's Extras.** When he was offered fifty dollars for the manuscript, he took it. He needed a new suit.

Later he came to regret having done so; sales of the book went into the millions, but he received no royalties. Henry Ford, whom Archibald had met at Steinmetz's house while at Union, gave the publication to his 25,000 workers. The Seventh Day Adventists distributed 10,000. Some schools presented a copy of **Life's Extras** to their graduating seniors.

With the Great Depression now over the land, and

Rutledge received the John Burroughs
Medal for best nature writing in 1930.

Archibald's sons of college age, money was badly needed. After selling off some heirloom furniture, Archibald
searched for other means of getting money. Being a
hunter, he had always kept a dog, and now his eyes fell
on his current one, Mike. Through the years the red-
and-yellow-haired bird dog had given him much
pleasure. Although his feet were large, which gave him a
funny-looking walk as if he wore snow shoes, he was
loyal and lovable.

Having seen him hunt, a man of means had approached Archibald several times to buy him. The
treasurer at Princeton where his three sons were
enrolled waited for payment. Archibald had no choice.

Feeling like a sinner, he built a crate to send Mike to
his new owner. When he had finished and put Mike into
it, the dog lay on the bottom of the box and looked at
his master with big misty eyes. Trying to avoid the eyes
of the bird dog, Archibald loaded the crate onto his
wheelbarrow and rolled it down to the express office. As
he began walking away, Archibald heard Mike
whimpering. It sounded to him as if the dog was weep-
ing.

Archibald had not yet reached home when the
magnitude of what he had done overcame him. He

rushed back to the express office. "It's a mistake!" he cried to the agent. "I'd like to get the dog back."

In 1930 in the midst of the Depression, Archibald's book **Peace in the Heart** and other writings received the John Burroughs Medal for "the best nature writing of the year." Dr. Van Dyke, his fishing companion, had recommended the book for this honor. Receiving this award not only brought Archibald great happiness, but increased demand for his writing.

On the eve of Archibald's departure to receive this medal, he was called on to speak to the boys at the Academy.

"For your sakes," he said, "I will try to look as intelligent as possible."

Always mindful that his talent for writing had come from God, he wrote "Fame."

> Of fame's austere
> Illustrious power
> He has the crown,
> He wears the flower,
> Who kindles fair,
> With fragile art,
> The flame of hope
> In a frozen heart.

Seventeen

Even though his parents had passed away, Archibald and his family continued to make their annual Christmas visits to Hampton. Each year Archibald became more convinced that if it were not for the faithfulness of Prince Alston's family who lived in the big kitchen in the yard, he could not have held on to the place he loved.

The Negroes looked after the big house, always putting it in order before a visit, planted some of the fields, and cared for the Rutledges when they came down from the North. They would open and air the plantation house, make the beds, and pile the wood boxes high with lightwood, scrub oak, and ash.

Eager in anticipation of the homecoming, they always had peanuts, eggs, sweet potatoes, and turkeys ready to exchange for the gifts the Rutledges brought from the North - hankerchiefs, beads, jewelry, coffee, tea, candy, and sugar.

On these trips away from the raucous cries of the street and the bedlam of motor horns, the memories of his parents were more alive than ever to Archibald.

He remembered how his father would give his
treasured pocket watch to him every time he came
home. And each time on the evening of his departure
Archibald would slip the family heirloom back in a little
top drawer of his father's mahogany dresser. He knew
how much the Colonel would miss the watch if he took
him up on his generous offer.

In a sense this repeated performance took on the sym-
bolism of a religious rite.

On one such visit to the plantation home the family
had gathered around the fire after dinner to talk, as was
their custom, when the Colonel left the room. Archibald
thought his father, now more distinguished looking
than ever with his gray mustache and long sideburns,
had gone for the watch. However, when his father
returned, he was not carrying the pocket watch but a
thin wooden matchbox.

He leaned over to Archibald, slid off the cover, and
with tender care placed the fragile box in Archibald's
hand. Inside was the track of a buck imbeded deeply in
hardened white sand.

"You remember, Arch," the Colonel said with a
twinkle in his eye, "how we used to smooth over deer
tracks so the pineland hunters wouldn't be able to track
down our deer and find them?"

Remembering, Archibald smiled.

"Well," his father continued, "I was on my way
home from the mail when I saw this track. It was so
fresh it was almost smoking, and I just couldn't bear for
you not to see it."

"But the matchbox?" Archibald asked, highly a-
mused. "How did you happen to have something to put
it in?"

Smile lines played around the Colonel's face as he
glanced at his wife. "Your mother had sent me for a

box of matches. You know the Lord provides so I emptied the matches in the floor of the buggy, ran my knife around the track, and lifted it into the empty box.''

Best of all, Archibald recalled the time when his father, after reading one of his poems published in **Scribners' Magazine,** wrote to him. ''Son,'' he had said, ''I was wrong not to encourage your writing. I am proud of you.''

The poem was ''Arrivals.''

> The child who leaves the mystic cradling
> Beneath his mother's heart, - how can he guess
> Of waiting true love's welcoming caress?
> What knowledge of his new world can he bring?
> What knows he of a mother's ministering?
> Yet love yearns over his mere helplessness,
> With strength to shield, with holy prayers to bless.
> With arms to hold, and tenderest voice to sing.
>
> So when his feet upon life's western slope
> Are setting toward that other land unknown,
> His heart shall be sustained by this sweet hope:
> That as to mortal days, naked, alone,
> Weeping he came, yet found love's welcome here,
> Solace no less than love's shall be his there.

Looking back, Archibald could understand his father's feelings. He had been a soldier, and having a son who wrote verse had not appealed to his soldier's heart. The Colonel had lived before the day when a man might write without being considered effeminate. Being the Colonel's son had always been a talisman for Archibald, and he had never felt any malice concerning his father's views. Until his father sent his apology, Archibald had never really realized just how much the Colonel's approval meant to him. And now, returning home to the spirit of his father, he was warmed by this remembrance.

The boys loved spending Christmas at Hampton so

much that the family continued to come. As they grew older, they fell under the same magic spell which the plantation had always held over their father. They loved to hunt in the woods and fields. They hunted with some of the same deer drivers their father had as a boy and with Prince's three sons.

It was on one of these Christmas visits that the idea of a Christmas Hunt began to take shape.

Riding to the hounds after the English fashion was a romantic and exciting sport. After all, wasn't Hampton named for Hampton Court Palace in England?

Most of the Christmases of Archibald's childhood had been quite memorable. A few had been rather bleak, especially one year in which a hurricane had destroyed the rice crop, Hampton's one source of income.

And now, with the planning of a Christmas Hunt, Archibald wanted to make this season a happy occasion for his sons and friends.

In contrast to snow-laden Pennsylvania, Christmas at Hampton had always been a green one, made so by pine, holly, myrtle, sweet bay, and smilax.

As in the days of his youth, every fireplace flamed with the wildwood fragrance of tupelo, elm, black gum, live oak, or sap pine.

During these times with the air of expectancy hovering everywhere, Archibald could almost see his mother moving about under the fragrant mistletoe.

Christmas breakfast was served on a table adorned with sprigs of holly, mistletoe, and ropes of smilax. Roasted mallards, venison sausage and crisp brown cornbread followed an earlier cup of tea and roll with marmalade.

Outside, the Negro huntsmen tuned up their hunting horns in anticipation of the magnificent stags whose tracks had been seen at deer crossings. These they had saved for the Christmas Hunt. Nearby the dogs stood with melancholy eyes.

Once they were astride their mounts, Archibald again felt the presence of the Colonel in regal carriage like an English sportsman.

Archibald led the procession as the hunters moved down the sandy road under moss-laden oaks. Even then they were on the lookout for deer tracks.

Through the sun-dappled tangle of greenery and pinelands they rode - thrilling to the deep-chested music of the hounds as they dashed over the knolls and dipped into the hollows.

Around dark the hunters returned. At the blowing of the horn the Negroes spilled from their cabins to fetch venison steaks.

Sue Alston stood ready to serve a royal dinner of the turkey Gabriel had killed on the delta, along with "hopping john," browned sweet potatoes with sugar oozing from their jackets, tenderloin of pork, pilau, and cardinal pudding.

After dinner everyone gathered in a semicircle before the fire. With old stags' heads gazing down on them, they rehunted the chases of the day.

When another Christmas Day at the plantation ended, Archibald moved out onto the broad porch of Hampton to see the stars and listen once more to the sweet singing of the Negroes.

With the live oaks shimmering in the moonlight and the sound of wild ducks' wings in the far sky, memories flooded over him. Peace filled his heart.

It was after just such a Hampton Christmas that Archibald lost his lost his beloved Florence. In January of 1934 she suffered a cerebral hemorrhage.

After lying in a coma for five days, "Aunt Dixie," as

she was called by her nieces, died. She was buried in Magnolia Cemetery in Charleston.

Gripped by the thoughts of love and death, Archibald wrote "Taj Mahal."

> When we appraise the harvest of our joys
> Transient they seem and meagre. It is willed
> Silence is barren when the laughter's stilled.
> If bliss makes aught, it is a fragile toy,
> That we in merriment may soon destroy.
> Out of our gladness little can be built;
> Felicity is in itself fulfilled.
> Not toward eternity delights deploy.
>
> Grief is the mighty builder and the wise.
> From anguish to illustrious beauty born,
> Out of life's darkness, towering for the morn,
> The glory of this fane ascends the skies.
> On majesty they made, we see them fall, -
> The eternal tears that wept the Taj Mahal.

This sonnet, written during the period of mourning for Florence, has been widely copied and translated. In seeking strength for his own sorrow, Archibald was able to give others comfort and hope. The gratitude he received in return was a comfort to him. "It is my faith," he wrote, "that compassion is the loveliest flower of the human spirit."

Eighteen

Still in the throes of grief from losing his wife, Archibald returned to Mercersburg to teach.

Dr. Boyd Edwards, then headmaster of the Academy, and his wife insisted that Archibald move into their home. He should not, they felt, be alone in his confused and desolate state, and the couple did all they could to comfort him.

Although 1934 proved to be a difficult year in Archibald's life, it became a memorable one, too. Working out of state, he had been quite unaware that South Carolina Governor Ibra C. Blackwood, with the approval of the legislature, had called for an appointment of some outstanding and distinguished man of letters to be named as the state's first poet laureate.

A telegram from his son Mid, then a medical student in Charleston, read:

> You have been appointed Poet Laureate by the Governor. Congratulations. Terribly proud. Love, Mid. March 3, 1934.

Later on the same day a letter from the governor's office arrived:

My dear Mr. Rutledge,

Governor Blackwood requests me to inform you that he has today, in recognition of your contribution to South Carolina literature, appointed you Poet Laureate of South Carolina.

Charles H. Gerard, Secretary

Newspapers carried accounts of South Carolina's gifted son's being chosen to fill a post recently created. The articles described Archibald as a devotee of outdoor life and told of his youth spent in an atmosphere of beauty on the family plantation on the Santee River, the locale of his many poems and nature stories.

On a short visit to Charleston to see his son Mid, reporters questioned Archibald about the possibility of returning to his native state to live.

"I cannot speak definitely at the present time," he said, "but there is a good possibility of my coming back to South Carolina as a full-time resident next year."

He did admit, however, that he always had returned home in his mind, and compared himself to an animal who returns home. Although he had now taught for thirty-three years at Mercersburg, he had always kept a warm place in his heart for Hampton and the Santee delta.

Archibald was deeply honored that he should receive this recognition, especially at a time when he was in Pennsylvania rather than a resident of South Carolina.

A year after being appointed South Carolina's poet laureate, Archibald sat reading a Pennsylvania newspaper. He could not believe what he saw. **Plans were being made to dam and divert the Santee River to generate power.**

Such a move would mean death to his beloved Santee delta and the wildlife that had always been such a part of him. No vegetation would be able to grow in the vast wasteland that would be created. Without the strong

*This portrait of Rutledge hangs in the
South Carolina House of Representatives
in honor of his many years as Poet
Laureate of the state.*

outward flow of the Santee River, salt water from the
ocean would flow in, killing plant life for at least sixty
miles inland. For it would be at that point the Santee
would be forced into the little Cooper River, a mere
wood stream that emptied into Charleston harbor.

Feverish in his attempts to save the land he had
roamed as a boy, Archibald began a campaign of letters
against the project. He wrote articles in an effort to
make the public aware of what would have to be given
up in order to use the rolling Santee for power.

Politicians who had worked to initiate the project
grew angry at Archibald's protests. Hadn't they given
him the honor of poet laureate of South Carolina? They
could surely take this honor away. No one, they felt,

who truly had the interest of his state at heart would want to hold back progress. And as far as this governing body was concerned, that was what Archibald Rutledge was trying to do.

But in his heart Archibald knew better. Sadly, he knew that the politicians were blind to what they would be doing to the beautiful Santee and the wildlife that had made it their home.

How could they know of the "marvelous voices atune with the dawn-wind"? And of how the "wind folds by the peace of the waters" and "the feet pausing in the woodland's bright calm"?

Was the entire country to be destroyed in the name of progress? Archibald grew desperate in his desire to preserve the land he loved. Friends supported his cause: some shared his fears of ecology; others defended his right to express his views without being penalized.

One young legislator who understood Archibald's love for the beauty of South Carolina spoke out on his behalf. This was Colonel John A. May from Aiken. Not only did he defeat the move to abolish the office of poet laureate, but he sponsored a House Resolution to express confidence in the distinguished service Archibald had rendered to his state. He pointed to Article I of the Constitution of the United States that provides freedom of speech and Article I, Section 4 that further guarantees free exercise of freedom of speech.

Thus, May commended Archibald for his efforts and expressed deep regret that such a move was made by the General Assembly. Several others joined in his support.

Although Archibald appreciated Colonel May's apology and vote of confidence, he realized that he could not stop the project to dam and divert the Santee River for hydroelectric power. In a few years the Santee delta of his boyhood would be only a memory.

Nineteen

Still in a period of unrest over losing Floy and of having to cope with the legislative decision to convert the Santee River for power, Archibald did what he had always done in times of stress. He turned his thoughts to his homeland, and the call to return became as intense as when he was a boy away for the first time.

His sons, Arch, Jr., Mid, and Irvine, were away from home now and their educations almost accomplished. If only . . . .

Along with the nostalgic reminiscing of returning to Hampton came renewed friendships. When in 1900 Archibald had gone North to college, he lost contact with many of his friends of his youth. One of these persons was Alice Lucas. She had been his childhood sweetheart when he rode horseback to Wedge Plantation for tutoring by her older sister. It was this teacher who had coined him "Wilful Archie."

A vivid memory of his love life at his young age had given him a chuckle through the years. At one point he had fallen violently in love with Belle Lofton, one of the village girls. Somehow, though, as the romance continued, the beauty of Alice Lucas kept edging itself into his mind and troubling him.

Finally he decided to "extricate himself honorably" from Belle. He had given her a tiny knife to "seal our troth," so when she returned it to him in a moment of anger, Archie breathed a sigh of relief. Now he could go back to Alice.

Go back to Alice was what he did now. Being with her after all these years and renewing old friendships gave him the comfort and feeling of belonging he needed. Before long he and Alice were married.

In the spring of 1937, after thirty-three years of teaching and being part-time registrar, Archibald was granted retirement benefits by Mercersburg Academy. At this time, too, the South Carolina Legislature began to pay him a stipend for services as poet laureate. With these two sources of income, he was able at last to return to the place he fondly called "The Lady of My Dreams."

Alice, used to the vigor of plantation life, was willing to return to Hampton with her husband. It would not bother her that there was no air conditioning, central heat, telephone, or, at that time, electricity.

Except for the Christmas visits, Hampton had been deserted for sixteen years since the Colonel's death.

On hearing of Archibald's plans, many friends tried to discourage him. "Deserted plantations are bought by millionaires who turn them into magnificent estates," they said. Archibald could understand their concern: the cost would be monstrous.

At fifty-three and in good health, Archibald knew what he had to do - follow his heart. To him there was no earthly loneliness worse than that of seeing the abandonment of a place once loved. To let Hampton go

Some years after the death of his first wife, Rutledge married Alice Lucas, his childhood sweetheart.

would be to lose his soul. The two-hundred-year heritage from the Rutledges and Horrys needed him.

Since coming North Archibald had watched a change in race relations, but still he knew that he could count on the Negroes of Hampton to help him in his enormous task. Many of them were descendants of the former slaves of the Rutledges' ancestors, and he knew them well. They possessed a high degree of faith, patience, and allegiance.

Hampton was a part of their way of life. They loved it and the Rutledge family, and Archibald loved them in the same manner his father had.

Thus, drawing on faith, hope, hard work, and most importantly, the loyalty of the Hampton Negroes, Archibald made plans to return home.

Twenty

In August of 1937 Archibald found the road to Hampton almost impassable. Vines, briars, tall weeds and overgrown bushes flourished beneath giant live oaks shrouded with Spanish moss. In spite of this, love burst in his heart. Not far beyond, his stately childhood home with its eight great pillars supporting the expansive portico awaited him.

After departing for school thirty-seven years earlier, he had returned for only short visits. But this time he had come home to stay. He would make his dream a reality: he would restore this 209-year-old Georgian country house to something of its beauty in 1730 when it was built by his ancestors.

Even though he had been away a long time, the two-thousand acre tract of land along the southern bank of the Santee had always been uppermost in this mind He was coming back to the scenes of his childhood. The magic of it all was still in his blood - the birds, animals, strange reptiles, and the lovely mystery of the river and swamp.

Hampton Plantation had suffered immensely from its being un-occupied for seven years. Inside, plaster was falling, and bushes and vines grew to its very steps.

No longer would there be fields of rice, level and golden, stretching between the broad rivers of the Santee and the Cooper in their flight to the sea. Instead, he would find a green wilderness of gloomy swamps of cypress trunks and towering pines - a place as primeval as it must have been in the days of the Indian.

The wasteland of the delta would be as it was in the days of his youth - a haunt for marsh rabbits, wild boar, deer, alligators, turkeys, blackbirds, and wild fowl. It would as always be frequented by migrating ducks. Besides the murky swampland, the woodlands still held yellow pine, black cypress, gum, tupelo, and water oak.

And now as Archibald drove up to the house, it looked as if someone had put a curse over it such as the one the wicked witch put on the house of the sleeping princess.

From the Washington Oak, gnarled and mighty, two stark limbs jutted skyward. Weeds, bushes, and briars spread to the very doors. Many were as high as Archibald's head.

Hadn't all his friends thought him foolhardy for returning? But then he had always liked the saying, "The difficult is what can be done now; the impossible, what can be done soon."

By the time he had switched off the motor of his car, a band of Negroes appeared from the side of the house. A glow of affection beamed on their faces.

The feeling of despair that had begun to slip over him at the sight of his beloved Hampton in such ruin began to lift. With such encouragement he could do anything.

And yet as he looked across the faces, some were missing - Martha Alston, their faithful cook, and her son Prince.

Painfully, Archibald remembered a trip home some years back. He had left in a drizzle of rain. His little Ford bulged with family members and reminders of Hampton. Luggage hung from both running boards. Farewells had already been said, so Archibald was surprised to see Prince run up to the driver's side of the car.

"Cap'n!" Prince called as he stood there with his battered cap in his hand. "Please, could you get out of the car a minute?"

Puzzled by his request, Archibald climbed head first from his wedged position.

Prince pulled him aside and looked at him squarely. "Please, Cap'n," he said, "take off your hat. I just want to look at your face one more time."

A short time later Archibald heard that Prince had died. Had he a premonition that they would not see each

Archibald and Prince, as young men, start out on a hunt. They were constant companions as children and remained friends even as adults.

other again? How many times had Archibald heard him answer a request with "All right, I will do it for you - if life lasts."

Life on the Santee delta had ceased to last for Prince Alston. With poignant memories Archibald thought of his dear friend lying in the Negro burial ground, where yellow jessamine rioted over azaleas, myrtles and dogwoods. He had left behind a host of mourners, a wife and three sons, one of whom carried his name. The loss of his childhood companion had also left a void in the heart of Archibald.

On his first night back Archibald had a hard time sleeping. Granted, he had come by way of an artery of traffic with ceaseless roar to the husband greenery of Hampton. But two horned owls had set up housekeeping in the Washington Oak. Their calls broke the silence of the night with weird sounds like that of dying music.

The next morning, however, Archibald was again enveloped with the magic of Hampton and turned to the task at hand.

Since early childhood he had always heard that Hampton was built by Noah Serre and left by will to his daughter Judith. This daughter had become the wife of Daniel Horry. After her death Horry married Harriet Pinckney, the daughter of Eliza Lucas.

Archibald was also told that he had descended from this lady who introduced indigo into South Carolina, and that she in her latter years had lived at Hampton with her daughter.

It had been extremely difficult, though, for him to get his lineage straight. His parents had told him that the brothers John and Edward Rutledge were both his ancestors. Yet he had a hard time remembering that the daughter of Daniel and Harriet Horry married Frederick Rutledge, John's son, and that their son Frederick married his second cousin Henrietta Rutledge, who was the daughter of Edward Rutledge. The Colonel had been born of that union.

Even though it became quite confusing, it had been fun to try to trace their family down through the Horrys and Pinckneys and Rutledges.

Archibald had been told, too, that the land on which Hampton was built was a grant from King George I. Thus the large rooms and high ceilings, as well as the bookcases lining the walls of the living room, were inspired by the English example.

During the Civil War Federal gunboats had come up the river and the rice barns had been destroyed, but fortunately, Hampton itself had not been touched.

Sometime earlier when Archibald had put a slate roof

on the house, the workers had uncovered seven roofs. It seemed that each time the house leaked, a new roof of cypress shingles had covered the old.

Most of the original furniture had by now been removed from the plantation. At his parents' death Archibald had encouraged his sisters to take what they wanted. Upon his decision to return, he bought out their rights in the homeplace, yet they knew Hampton would always be home to them.

For days he and his helpers went through the fourteen-room house and the seven cellars beneath it trying to determine where to begin in the Herculean task of restoration.

First they installed a new heater system and painted the six rooms on the first floor.

The most ambitious of tasks was the restoration of the ballroom. With help, Archibald hewed down cypress poles from the nearby riverbank and made a platform from which to scrape and paint the beautiful fully arched 28-foot ceiling.

The fireplace in the ballroom, more than seven feet wide and faced on either side with colorful Delft tiles, held a special affection for him. He loved the scenes which ranged from pagan to biblical.

While he worked, happy memories of playing in the grand room as a child came back to him. With a smile he thought of the day he, Tom, and Prince had turned over the ballroom to the birds.

Diligently Archibald and his faithful workers labored from the top of the house to the arches of the cellars. Imbedded in the ceilings of these cellars were castiron hooks probably used for storing cured hams. The cellar area beneath the front portico had been paved with broad brick, but now they were covered with a deposit of silt and sand a foot deep.

Underneath the house Archibald dug up an assortment of relics: broken Wedgewood china; old brass locks, hinges and keys; and hand-blown bottles. The best find was twenty-eight Delft tiles resembling those in the ballroom fireplace.

In fact, Archibald found so many relics about the plantation that he decided to make a museum in the huge old front room of the outside kitchen. During his boyhood, food had been cooked in this separate house using the cavernous fireplace with Dutch ovens and spits. Now it would serve as a place for visitors to view treasured relics.

Realizing that everyone did not appreciate hunting trophies as he did, Archibald set aside a back room upstairs as a trophy room. There he assembled his large collection that at one time had adorned the hallway and rooms throughout the house. More than three hundred sets of deer antlers and other relics of the wilds were placed in the trophy room. Included were the largest antlers ever taken in the southeastern United States and record racks for various species in South Carolina.

Visitors to Hampton had found it puzzling that four flights of mahogany stairs at the back of the house rose from the first floor to the attic. Archibald explained to them that in the old days almost all travel between plantations was by water. Therefore, the side that faced the river could also be considered the front.

Even though Archibald was an adult, an aura of mystery still hung about the secret closet in the house, and especially about the hollow section on the right of it that had been closed since before he was born.

From the cellar under the ballroom, Archibald and a companion, Lewis Colleton, sawed through the floor and into the mysterious compartment.

When the black chasm appeared above them, Lewis'

superstition became such that Archibald lost him for the rest of the day.

Archibald climbed into the hollow well alone. The glow of his flashlight picked up dust and spiderwebs and then a small box. Inside was a piece of paper with the plan of a house which he recognized as Hampton. From one corner a line moved to a marked spot. By this spot was the drawing of a shovel.

Now his curiosity was really aroused. He moved outside, all the while following the map in his hand. On the exact spot shown on the map grew a century-old oak. His curiosity had not been satisfied after all. Had someone long ago buried something there and planted a tree to mark the spot? If so, then it would remain a mystery, for the roots of such a giant oak could not be moved. Whether or not a treasure waited, he would never know.

But coming home meant more to Archibald than buried treasure. When springtime arrived, his heart welled once more to the magic of nature. The fragrant black loam heaved behind plows. Among the furrows wild flowers flourished.

It did not matter to him that, not being a millionaire, he could not afford to have others restore Hampton in the grand fashion of its earlier days. The wealth he had was far greater. He expressed his feelings in "Vast Empire."

> Let me not envy those
> Who heap their treasures high;
> My realm is wide and deep.
> Let me but love a rose,
> Or a blue reach of sky,
> And it is mine to keep.
>
> The mountain and the main,
> The shaggy forest old
> Are mine for loving them.

And mine the glimmering plain,
The sunset's fount of gold,
The stars, dark's diadem.

The birds' pure wildwood songs
Are of my wealth a part,
Misfortune to beguile.
Beauty to him belongs
Who holds it in his heart,
Worshiping all the while.

Since the plantation Negroes' schoolhouse was only a short distance away, Archibald hired the children to help beautify the grounds.

Moving from group to group, he warned them to beware of snakes, for he had already killed four copperheads and two coral snakes, the latter so brilliant he told the children they look like dimestore necklaces.

Along with clearing unwanted bushes, Archibald planted avenues of holly and dogwood. From cuttings he began more camellia japonicas.

Each day Hampton grew all the more beautiful.

Since the weather was warm, deerflies and mosquitoes made it necessary for him to take quinine to ward of malaria. In spite of this, he was glad that he no longer was timed by bells but awoke to the cheerful call of birds.

As always yellow jessamine and red woodbine decorated the woods. The Pride of India tree arrayed herself in purple, and the traveler's joy hung in lavender stalactites.

Along the swamp edges lilies glimmered; the nightshade hung her purple lamps; and wild azaleas and dogwoods starred the forest with their blooms.

A tall figure in a tattered hunting coat walked down a narrow dirt path among the shadows and patches of sunlight.

Archibald was truly home.

Twenty-One

Although it was good to be home, Archibald found many changes. One was the lack of ducks on the plantation. When he was a boy, duck hunting had been a favorite sport on the delta. People had come from all over to hunt there.

It always gave Archibald great pleasure to remember when as a lad he led President Grover Cleveland to his duck blind. President Cleveland was a great duck hunter, but he was so heavy he found it difficult to shift his weight around in an ordinary box in the blind. To accommodate him, a piano stool was mounted on a wide platform.

In the twilight of the morning Archibald led him down a dim rice field bank. President Cleveland talked in a jovial fashion all the way. The path crossed a broad, deep canal half filled with muddy water. Because of the President's enormous size, a wide, thick cypress board had been placed across the canal.

Archibald warned him to be careful, but the President kept talking away, missed the board with one foot, and plunged headlong into the muddy water.

The guide waiting at the duck blind heard the commotion and came to the rescue.

The President was a good sport, however. He took all the blame, and that night at the clubhouse he brought roars of laughter with the tale.

Now Archibald could see the ducks flying up and down the river by the thousands: mallards, black ducks, teal, widgeons, and scaups. Yet they did not light on his place.

With this knowledge of wildlife, he knew the problem. Rice was no longer grown at Hampton, and the banks of former rice fields had been broken by the tides. Salt water from the sea had now ruined the delta. The fields had grown up wild, and water flowed and ebbed at will. He knew, too, that ducks look for shallow water for feeding. They do not dive but feed "tipping up."

Just after the closing of duck season in late December, Archibald began to prepare a field for ducks. With the help of the Negroes he put in a spillway and repaired an old bank. Then he directed a little wood stream into the field. Once that had been completed, he and his companions planted birches and alders on the bank to hold it.

Within a short while great flocks of ducks were coming to the field. Every afternoon they came. At night Archibald could hear them in the marsh and duck oats. Every morning just before sunrise they left.

Many other wild animals also found the lake a convenient home - bass, bream, alligators, and snowy egrets.

Of all the phenomena of nature, that of migration had always made the most profound impression on Archibald. While the vast expanse of country to the north was still blizzard-bound, with icy winds and bare boughs, the clanging chorus of wild geese filled the air.

Even in the darkness the air tingled with their communication.

Each winged creature, the geese and mallards, followed a familiar path. Along the way they encouraged each other, stopping now and then as at Hampton to rest from their flights and to don new plumage. Some selected mates.

Continuing his lifetime habit of being out of the house before daybreak, Archibald took early mornings to watch for small birds like the ruby-throated hummingbird with its gossamer wings and the pitifully frail grebe. He also watched for the large ones - the whistling swan and the wide-winged egret. They filled the woods and the solitary marshes with their song.

Among these troubadours of spring the most fascinating to him became the Baltimore oriole. "Like a gorgeous autumn leaf he flits from bough to bough," he wrote. The male orioles arrived first, "their brilliant firebrands burning against the leafing tree," and they departed before the females came.

With these harbingers of spring, the wild and the beautiful found a voice in tune with Archibald's own heart.

Even though the wildlife and the restoration of Hampton offered Archibald much pleasure, he missed many of the conveniences he had been accustomed to in Pennsylvania. For one thing, Hampton still had no electricity. Also, the nearest store was fifteen miles away. Because of this, it became necessary for the Rutledges to plant a garden. Since the freshets brought silt to the Santee, having a fertile land was no problem. The land, for the most part, now became their livelihood.

Mrs. Rutledge might say, "We have nothing for dinner."

Then Archibald would fill his roomy coat pocket with

Archibald and his three sons (from left to right): Archibald, Jr.,
Henry Middleton and Irvine Hart.

shells, take the English Daly his sons had given him, and
go look for wild game for dinner. Sometimes he had to
go no farther than the front gate as the deer came up to
the yard. Even on the rare occasions when he did not
have hunter's luck, he would never venture to the island
he had set aside as a game sanctuary.

Another problem was that of the freshets. Since so
many forests had been cut in the Piedmont region of
South Carolina and in western North Carolina, heavy
rains raced into the rivers. Bare hills did not absorb the
water as those covered with leaf mold and pine straw
had done. Thus, coastal areas were sometimes flooded.

As early as 1915 rice growing had ceased in South Carolina because of these floods or freshets. Plantation owners might have a thousand acres of ripe rice when a freshet out of the northwest would disrupt the whole system of dikes and floodgates.

Not only was the year's investment gone, but the environmental damage was great. In his boyhood Archibald had seen a thirty-foot flood. It had destroyed the rice as well as put all the stock in the Low Country in peril.

After the Great Gale in 1822 that had drowned many workers in the rice fields, solitary brick towers had been built as places of refuge. They reached thirty feet with inside staircases and a platform on top. These circular brick structures resembled miniature lighthouses on the rice fields. Although most of them had been demolished for use of the brick, Archibald could still see their remnants along the waterways. They made him think of the old woman who had once told him that she had been born "in one of them slave towers on Wicklow."

Fortunately, bulletins warned of such rainfall about a week before the freshet reached the Santee, for water at Hampton would rise anywhere from five to twelve feet.

While houses had been built on the delta for the slaves and their overseers, the plantation homes were always on the mainland on bluffs above the river. The builders of Hampton had protected it from rising water by placing it on high ground.

It was easy, too, to tell when a freshet was in the making, for cries of alarm came from wild things. Nature in a rampage charged the air with an ominous feeling. A peculiar noise, a sort of hissed whisper, rustled in the submerged marsh. Now and then wild, murkey, debris-choked water plunged through a spillway, or a breaking dam roared.

At such a time one day in March, Archibald ventured out in his canoe. The yellow jessamine had begun to bloom and a myriad of migrating birds flocked in the sky. The tender green of spring touched the myrtles.

Yet Archibald dared not extend a hand to touch the greenery, for he knew rattlers or cottonmouth moccasins might be stretched out on low limbs.

Not far from him a drifting log carried a king rail and two swamp rabbits.

"Floods make strange bed fellows," Archibald thought as he viewed the companions seeking safety.

Paddling into the swamp, he heard a tremendous splash. Three deer swam away from a pile of logs where they had been marooned. Archibald knew they were headed for Pine Ridge, always the last spot to be covered by a flood.

He dared not land his canoe. Copperheads and moccasins, and perhaps a diamondback, had been washed out of hibernation close by. Although groggy and sluggish, they were still deadly.

Even animals who missed the chance to forage, like Wilson's snipe, woodcocks, swamp rabbits, and gray squirrels, managed well in the freshets.

After several days when the water began to recede, it took with it to the ocean all that would float - logs, stray boats, chicken coops, and a vast array of flotsam.

On this refuse much wildlife washed out to sea. Later on much of the debris littered the beaches of the coastal islands.

After such an experience Archibald turned homeward. Along the way he noted that every fern and flower was lost under the yellow water of the now drowned swamp lands. Yet his heart was at peace, for he knew that all this would pass and that life and resurrection and beauty are eternal.

Twenty-Two

Not long after his return to Hampton, Archibald had an article published in **The Saturday Evening Post.** Called "Return of the Native," it created much interest in Hampton Plantation. So much so, in fact, that he began expanding it into a book, **Home by the River.** In it he told the history of famous Hampton, of the treasures found in restoration, of repainting the house, and of refinishing the ballroom. He also related the interesting tales of the Negroes of the plantation.

Most importantly, he wrote in picturesque detail of the plantation at night, the time when the "raucous grunts of blue herons with their ponderous grace answer each other in the heavens" and when "the woods are suffused with lilac, orchid and rosy lights, and the day dies in beauty." He put the reader there with him among the purple-topped pines as he "accepts life as a privilege to be in communion with beauty and with ancient order and the eternal rhythm of creation."

Then when the "light has faded on the misty and glimmering brakes," the reader moves with him through the starlight until the night awakes in loveliness. The woods rustle under the movements of nocturnal animals, and moonlight brings its transfiguring power to the woods, "statuing every object in lily-white marble."

Lovers of romantic history and wildlife reveled in **Home by the River,** his most popular publication.

In the book Archibald said strangers were welcomed at Hampton. Those who read it took him up on the invitation, and soon a flow of travelers came to see Hampton and to meet the author. They were never disappointed, for they found Alice and Archibald patient and gracious listeners.

On one of these visits guests were about to leave by the front entrance when Mrs. Rutledge touched her husband's arm and whispered, "We'll have to go out the back way. The birds are feeding now."

Surely enough, half of the great front porch was covered with brilliant-colored birds feeding on cracked corn. The portico of stately Hampton had become a feeding station.

As they turned toward the back door, Archibald recalled the time during his childhood when a house wren built a nest in the front hall wicker basket the Rutledges used for gloves. They were unable to use the front entrance until the babies hatched.

About this time Hampton was featured in **National Geographic,** and before long Edward R. Murrow aired Hampton and its owners on national television.

Fans who could not come to Hampton wrote to Rutledge, and his cordial replies turned hundreds into devoted friends.

Meanwhile Archibald continued to enjoy the restoration of Hampton. He spent many hours poring over old trunks with letters and papers about Hampton. Although the papers were yellowed with age and the ornate handwriting was often hard to decipher, he read hundreds of them. As he did so, he could picture the early glamour of the plantation.

During the Revolution, especially after Charleston was captured by the British, Hampton became a place of refuge from the city.

"There are twenty-six of us here now," one letter read.

A letter that had always been treasured in his family was one from George Washington to Archibald's great-great-grandmother, Eliza Lucas Pinckney.

Still some forty miles from Hampton, he wanted to let his hostess know the approximate time of his arrival. He sent a night rider who had to cross the Pee Dee, the Black, the Sampit, and the Santee rivers before arriving at Hampton. When he finally arrived, the rider and the occupants of Hampton had chuckled over Washington's scrawled postscript on the letter. "For God's sake," it said, "give my rider some grog!"

Archibald had no doubt that the lonely rider was cheered by wine from a cellar of Hampton.

Looking through the old letters and papers, Archibald was reminded, too, of other famous people who had come to Hampton - Daniel Webster, Edgar Allan Poe, Robert E. Lee, and John James Audubon, the ornithologist who had painted birds of the Low Country. It seemed to Archibald that these illustrious guests lent Hampton a kind of dignity, and he had always been proudly impressed by this.

Letters dated in the time just after the Civil War spoke of persons' being required to take oaths not to bear arms against the Union before they could receive rents. One letter lamented the fact that some families had done so. "The taking of the oath was a bitter pill to Aunt Harriott," one letter read.

Archibald had always known that some of his family regarded him with unrestrained adoration and awe, yet finding a letter his older sister had written to their mother was a sharp reminder of her opinion of him. The letter had to do with Archibald's opposition to his sister's marriage. "Pay no attention to Archie," it said, "all of us know he is crazy."

The cutting remarks brought back the sharp tongue of another relative - Aunt Elise, his father's sister, who at the age of sixty looked like a Dresden vase. When at thirteen Archibald had some verse published in a magazine, Aunt Elise felt herself a worthy critic since she had something of a literary talent.

"Someday," she had written Archibald in her spidery hand, "a real critic will take you by the back of the neck and throw you as a dog shakes a rat far beyond the bounds of literature."

After Archibald was grown and had a family, he took one of his sons to visit his aunt. "Middleton," she said, "you will not like me. You see, I am the acrimonious member of the family."

Nevertheless, Aunt Elise could be sweet of heart, and Archibald felt he had learned something from her. Everyone, he felt, must come to an understanding that there are some people from whom a person can never expect any understanding or love. The important thing is not to be embittered by this disillusion but to use it to gain independence and perhaps stability of character.

When, however, **The Colonel and His Lady,** a book about Archibald's parents, was published, Aunt Elise had no criticism. Booth Tarkington called it a "classic of the South." **The New York Times** and other newspapers over the country praised it. **The Cleveland Press** said, "A writer who can bring a man to life, and make him live in the reader's very heart so that the reader knows and loves and respects him with a glowing suffused warmth - a writer who can do that must 'have something.' What that something is, Archibald Rutledge has. I strongly suspect it is genius.''

Regardless of any unpleasantness Archibald encountered, the charm of the springtime plantation with its snowy spirea, yellow jessamine, and red woodbine soothed his spirits. After finding renewed strength and peace in his wilderness retreat, he expressed his feelings in the poem ''In a Forest.''

> An orchestra with harps of gold
> Makes music in this forest old:
> I hear from dewy hill-hung firs
> Dim melodies of dulcimers;
> The regal cardinal is tall
> Carols a scarlet madrigal;
> The trumpets of the hidden stream
> Are silver horns heard in a dream;
> The wind's soft wand of lyric fire
> Touches the copse into a choir;
> The vireo 'mid the bloomy sprays
> Fingers the flute Titania plays:
> Such melody, surpassing art,
> Brings deepest silence to my heart.
>
> Then comes a quiet to the wood
> As if it uttered solitude.
> Demurely down the silent glade
> Shimmers the reticence of shade;
> Bright hauteurs virginally gleam
> From cloistered oaks, from soundless stream;
> A wild forsaken beauty shines
> About the hushed momentous pines;
> I did not dream that there could be
> Such stillness of felicity.
> The forest glimmers, mystic, mute. -
> A veiled enchantress. . . There's no lute,
> No harp, no cymbal, and no singing,
> But in my heart wild bells are ringing.

From these woods that offered him solace he brought up violets, lilies, and wild azaleas and planted them around the house. With each season Hampton grew more beautiful. Through the years Archibald had commented, "I was born to a civilization that had passed." Never did he feel this more acutely than when he engaged in nostalgic reminiscing. Yet he was glad that his father, and he after him, had been able to hold the title to Hampton.

Not only did retaining this beloved home mean a great deal to Archibald but to his sons. They continued to come with their families for vacations and the Christmas Hunts. By now neighboring plantations had begun hunts, too, and the owners vied with one another over their packs of hounds which, when hunted, sounded like matched chimney bells.

Alice put up good-naturedly with all the talk of hunting, and along with Archibald she enjoyed the grandchildren as the sons' families grew. It would be 1956 before she would have the comforts of electricity at Hampton, however.

No longer did Archibald have to worry about dressing up. He had always said a dress suit made him look alarmingly like a mule peering over a white-washed fence. Now he could look and feel natural in his hunting clothes.

In a short verse he drew his sentiments about being back at Hampton.

As azure is to the eagle,
As to the ship the sea,
As to the deer the wildwood,
So are you home to me.

Twenty-Three

While Archibald's **Home by the River,** his poetry, and stories of hunting and wildlife attracted many readers and brought praise from literary critics, he was enjoying Hampton Plantation. Still, he found time to write and to keep up a continuous flow of letters with his sons as well as admiring readers.

One day just as he had settled at his desk, Will Alston, grandson of his childhood friend Prince, and now the foreman of Hampton, appeared at the door.

"Cap'n," he said when Archibald answered his call, "sompin's got to be done 'bout dat great crocodile what swim up and down the river."

Archibald knew the problem. The monster had through the years killed dogs, hogs, ducks, and numerous wildlife in his long murderous career. Because alligators have such a long life span, some even more than a hundred years, the Negroes often were superstitious about them. Consequently, Archibald knew he could not count on much help in getting rid of the terror of Wambaw Creek.

Through the years he had often seen the old bull alligator in the water, and once he had seen him on the land. Unlike most alligators, he was jet black. Worst still, Archibald knew of the dark and forbidding cavern he had hollowed for himself on the bank of the river. There he took the bodies of creatures he killed, for he would not eat them until they were in condition to suit his taste.

Occasionally the scaly brute gave a resounding roar - one of the wildest and most primeval sounds in all nature.

Archibald never heard the roar of an alligator without remembering a time when he and Prince were about five years old. Mrs. Rutledge had given orders to stay out of the garden, but the delicious red strawberries were just too tempting.

Their mouths and hands were stained with red from the berries when the boys heard something that began as a thunderous moan and ended as a bellow.

"W'ah dat?" Prince asked, his eyes wide and his hands dropping the berries.

"What?" Archie asked as Prince answered his own question: **"Dat is de Debil."**

With juice still moist on their fingers, the boys flew in terror to Mrs. Rutledge.

It was not until years afterwards that they learned the weird moaning was made by a bull alligator.

Indeed, Archibald knew full well what kind of monster he was dealing with. Hadn't he seen a dog crushed with the mighty jaws of an alligator? As a boy he'd been hunting when his hound swam after a buck across a wide river. Just as the dog entered the water, Archibald saw an alligator lying close by. Nothing was showing but the tip of his nose and the periscopes of his eyes.

The living submarine, being a good judge of distance, did not move until the dog was too far out in the water to get back to shore before he reached him. Then he went after him like a torpedo, maneuvering his big body to the side of the helpless hound and closing in.

Archibald had brooded for days over the brutal death of his dog, and the Negroes had offered comfort by telling other dog-alligator tales.

Scipio, one of the few Negro alligator hunters, cautioned never to chain a dog near a place an alligator haunts. He took Archie down to some old cypress trees on the riverbank, and with the two of them hiding, he set up a whining series of barks like a cur dog treeing a squirrel.

Before long the ridge of a great spine and the top of a head with protruding eye sockets came above the murky waters. That happened, Scipio told him, because a dog is the favorite meat of the alligator. He also said that the cunning animal will often attack a dog while he is treeing another animal, unaware of the danger lurking close by.

Archibald knew, too, that on land the gator is awkward because his legs are not strong enough to support his weight, but in water he is streamlined.

In times of drought when frogs, turtles, and other water animals bury themselves in the moss and mud, an alligator will move overland to the river or to some other lake to find water.

From his boyhood Archibald remembered such a one - the alligator of Witch Pond, they called him. Moving around from one body of water to another, he had become a menace to the livestock in the area. Due to the dense thicket surrounding Witch Pond, any attempt to stalk the big brute was foiled by the noise created in trying to get near the pond. Every time Archie tried, the cracking of dry branches would give him away; the old gator would slip off the log where he sunned before Archie could get within a good shooting range of him.

In order to outwit the alligator, Archie decided to wade a shallow stream that fed into Witch Pond. By doing this he would move right up to the monster without being heard. Too, he would be shielded somewhat by the bald cypress growing in the pond.

The first part of his plan worked. He wound up the little ditch-like stream until he reached the lagoon where the old scaly bulk snoozed on his log in the spring sunshine.

By now Archie was in water up to his waist. He lifted his rifle. He was within range, but the cypress trees growing in the water stood in the way of a shot.

Besides, to kill an alligator he must be hit in the head or behind the foreshoulder, and neither of those vital spots was visible to Archie. Anywhere else the shot would not penetrate his flinty armor.

Not ready to give up, Archie had moved through the water toward the drowsing creature. With each step the soft mud bubbled and oozed beneath his feet.

The alligator had not stirred. Again Archie raised his rifle.

He happened to glance behind him. To his horror another alligator, even larger than the one on the log, lay behind him like a half-submerged submarine. **While he had been stalking the first alligator, he himself had been stalked.**

Archie fired his rifle at the alligator's head and dashed wildly for the shore.

Once on the safety of the bank he turned to see what had happened. Where the first monster had been lying, the water rocked with waves made by his sudden plunge.

Near the shore, turning in blind circles, was the grim stalker.

Archie shot once again and hit his target. A feeling of relief surged through him.

Later, with the help of Tom and Prince, Archie had pulled the dead alligator ashore. He measured almost fourteen feet long and weighed 1,100 pounds.

Now as Archibald prepared to catch the alligator in the creek behind Hampton, he knew that he would not be able to bring him out to shoot him unless he could hook him.

Once he and Prince had hooked a bull alligator known as "the great Jackfield bull." He had been given the name because he used to roar his grim solos in Jackfield, one of the lonely stretches on the delta.

They had led him on a line more than a mile down a reed-hung rice bank. Every so often the scaly monster would rise on his legs and rush at them.

Through the years Archibald had learned much about the alligator. He knew that his mouth was cavernous but not his throat. Because of that, a hook had to be just right.

Knowing all this, he began to make plans. Although in his boyhood he had used wooden hooks, he now got two sturdy sea bass hooks and fastened them to two strong dog chains to form a line that could not be bitten through.

To the other end of the chain he attached a hundred and fifty feet of hemp rope.

When the line was rigged, Archibald drove to a little country store and found a ham that was "going out of circulation," for alligators prefer meat that is decaying.

At home he split the ham and set the hooks in the groove. He then tied fishing cord around and around the ham.

Feeling this powerful animal could not be handled from his small boat, Archibald tied the line to a stout swamp oak near the wharf.

The next morning Archibald found the rope taut. He knew what that meant. As he began to pull on the rope, the waters erupted and the monstrous creature threw himself out of the water and fell back, jerking the rope from Archibald's hands.

Archibald hurried to the house for his rifle. Then he called Will to come and bring his six sons. Besides needing their help, he wanted the boys to have the experience of hauling in the hoary old monster.

As they pulled, the alligator would break water about every twenty feet. Every time the monster came closer, Archibald saw the fearful expressions of the boys. A live alligator could be dangerous on land, too, for his tail was as strong as his jaws. The fierce creature was known to strike a victim down with his tail and then seize it in his grim jaws.

A great crowd had gathered along the shore now, but no one wanted to be too close when the monster was pulled in.

Finally he was exposed enough that Archibald was able to shoot, and with great effort they pulled him ashore.

Will and his sons heaved and hauled until they got the fourteen-foot brute onto an old truck.

That night a party with roasted alligator meat celebrated the capture of the old bull alligator that had been feared so long. No longer would he keep in mortal terror the gentle and beautiful wild creatures of Hampton Plantation.

Twenty-Four

With his parents' interest in the outdoors, it would have been strange indeed if Archibald had not loved nature. Yet as he moved about the plantation, he was ever aware of others who had made a profound impression on him. Much of his writing attributed a great part of his attitude toward life to the Negroes of the plantation.

In 1928 **American Magazine** had published an article, "My Debt to Prince," and in December 1939 **The Saturday Evening Post** published, "It's a Dark Business but a Happy One if You Understand the Plantation Negro." In the latter he portrayed the wit and unpredictability of his black friends.

Among the books dedicated to these loyal companions was **Wildlife of the South,** published in 1935 and inscribed to his childhood companion Prince Alston. In November 1943 **Reader's Digest** also published his profile on Prince in its department, "The Most Unforgettable Character I've Met."

Oddly enough, most of the Negroes never cared for the delta, especially at night. Although they recognized its beauty and wild charm, the occult and mystery associated with the area overshadowed the beauty. Somehow their psychic powers seemed to come from the unwelcomed intimacy with darkness. So weird were the wildlife calls and screams heard from the delta that it was only natural for them to believe it to be the habitat of "hants" and "hobgoblins."

Once Archibald saw a Negro stop working in the garden because he'd heard a horned owl - a sign of the supernatural.

And there was a black-horned buck that because of his ability to escape hunters had become a sign of bad luck. Neither was it easy to forget that Amos Boykin, one of the best of the woodsmen, had vanished on a trip to the delta.

Yet the plantation Negro had a deep respect for nature. Their appreciation for the fading glory of a sunset or a new moon became Archie's, for, he noted, they never failed to pause in reverence to say "God bless the new moon."

As a boy he had watched an old Negro named Morris as he polished silver and cutlery in the plantation kitchen. It was this man who taught Archie that real suffering has the aspect of eternal things.

"I got a glory," he would say, for he knew that to find a glory and give it the strength that might be spent in despair was the only way out of suffering.

Perhaps none of the Negroes of Hampton was wiser than Galboa. He had been born in Africa and spoke more African than English. A former slave, he was close to the Colonel, and they often sat in the evening under the oaks outside the cabin the Colonel had built for him. He was a very old man when Archie was a boy, but in his younger days he had been the plantation fisherman.

Many times as a child Archie would be sent to

Gabe Myers taught Archie how to catch a fox with a buried sweet potato.

Galboa's cabin with the message, "Galboa, we need a wild turkey for Sunday" or "We need two rockfish for Wednesday."

"If you want to get game and fish," the old man would advise, "you must hunt with your head."

Archie remembered asking him whether he liked summer or winter best. He had answered, "I thank God for both."

And there was old Gabe Myers, who taught Archie that the easiest way to catch a fox was to bury a sweet potato in the ground. When Gabe lost his house to fire, Archibald had gone down to see him. Gabe and his family had moved into a tiny stable nearby.

"I saved one shirt," Gabe said, and a grin passed over his face. "And dat one is raggety."

"Well," Archibald had replied, "that's enough to make you sure enough depressed."

"Oh, I ain't got dat," Gabe assured him. "I ain't got the real depression 'cause I still got hope."

From this man Archie had learned that spiritual loss is the only real loss.

Archibald loved to tell of the old Negro who, anxious to end their conversation and get to prayer meeting, said, "Now I must go and light my candle at His fire."

Many a Rutledge verse was lighted at this same fire.

"Among them all," Archibald said, "the milk of human kindness runs deep, and it overflows in the softness of their voices and the genuineness of their handshakes. Their children live close to the life of the field and forest, the birds and animals and plants. Though they are young, they are wise with ancient wisdom. Their beautiful voices have in them the tones of the plantation birds.

"I would not take anything for what they have taught me," he said, "not the least thing being an equanimity that can come only from the grace of heart."

Best of all, there was Prince, who shared with him a thousand plantation adventures. No other person had the knack with animals that Prince Alston possessed.

In college Archibald had a course in practical psychology and another in animal psychology, but he had been helpless while Prince, without being formally taught, knew just what to do. Archie had seen him relate with dogs that were of the worst temperament.

One time Archie and Prince had taken Blossom, a strange new hound, into the woods for a ramble. The dog had refused to pay Archie the slightest attention, and Archie shamelessly turned him over to Prince.

Headstrong Blossom would race pell-mell after any scent that her delicate nostrils detected in the damp sandy soil.

Since they were in wild country unfamiliar to her, Archie started to suggest that they put Blossom on a leash so she would not get lost. But before he had a chance to do so, she sniffed a fresh buck track and left the road on a dead run.

Prince shouted; Blossom halted and turned.

"Blossom!" Prince called, then softening his voice

almost to a whisper, "Come here, chile. Here, Blossom, come here to me. You is the pretties', fines', mos' 'bedient houn' I ever did see." Step by crawling step Blossom approached Prince.

"That's a good girl; come on now," he coaxed. "Come on, Honey Blossom. I know you wouldn't leave me here in the road all by myself."

Completely taken by Prince's voice, she ran and leaped up on him and licked his hand.

Archie remembered, too, the first time he ever saw Prince charm a stubborn mule. As teenagers the two of them had been in a seacoast village not far from Hampton.

Nearby a farmer's mule stood harnessed to a wagon heavily loaded with Saturday's purchases. The animal had balked between the post office and the general store. Men who usually loafed on the sandy streets of the small town gathered around and offered advice.

Upon this advice the mule had been beaten and cursed, his harness removed, and the wagon rolled back. The owners had even resorted to building a small fire under him, but still the mule would not budge.

Archie watched while Prince approached the animal with gentle assurance and placed an affectionate arm around the animal's neck. Then he put his mouth very close to the mule's left ear and whispered something.

Instantly the mule relaxed and stepped forward.

On the way home Archie had asked Prince what he had said to the mule, but Prince had only laughed, for he never seemed to take his magic with animals seriously.

Too, Archibald enjoyed the way the Negroes made a lark out of their tasks. They did not like working alone, for together they kept up a continuous teasing and happy banter.

Above all, he appreciated their understanding. He remembered once when he had come home to Hampton during school holidays. He and a Negro companion Richard were hunting on Bull's Island, now a game preserve on the Carolina coast.

They had taken up the trail of a stag whose tracks indicated that his head would indeed be a prize trophy.

All day long through palmetto thickets, marshes and jungles of pine and oak they tracked him.

Near sundown they wove in and out of the shadows of the forest to the sand dunes along the coast. To their amazement the great stag stood poised in the twilight on the crest of a tawny dune.

Richard squatted out of the animal's view as Archibald readied his gun for the shot.

The statuesque stag stood silhouetted with the golden twilight fringing him. Behind him sea breakers foamed gently toward the shore.

Archibald leveled the sight of his gun on the deer's heart. Then slowly he lowered the gun from his shoulder and turned to his companion.

"Richard," he said apologetically, "I can't shoot him. The world is too beautiful."

"Young Cap'n," Richard said in his most gentle voice, "You know, sah, angels walk in the moonlight."

Archibald was grateful that Richard had understood why he could not kill the beautiful creature.

From his earliest childhood he had only pleasant memories of the Negroes' deep understanding of human nature as well as their friendship and devotion.

Being back at Hampton refreshed this sense of appreciation. Here there were no raucous cries of the street, no bedlam of motor horns, or the crackling of riveters - here there was only the heart's gentle resignation to a simple life.

Twenty-Five

For thirty years after Alice and Archibald returned home, he continued to restore Hampton, he wrote, lectured, planted in the soil he loved, welcomed his family home, and entertained the visitors who beat a path to his door.

His publications of poetry and prose were nearing the one hundred mark. **The Heart's Citadel, Beauty in the Heart, Brimming Tide, Those Were the Days, Santee Paradise, From the Hills to the Sea, Deep River,** and **Ballad of the Howling Hounds** came in close succession.

Published in 1960, **Deep River** is a complete collection of his poems. The book won six national awards and a gold cup from the International Poetry Society. It also made him a candidate for the Pulitzer Prize.

Critics hailed the poetry as having "deep perception, human tenderness, and a genius for expression." One said Rutledge's poem "Chant a la Mort" excels "Thanatopsis." Another, "Requiem," is a gem. "The Dreaming Mast," telling the dreams of a tree taken to be the mainmast for a vessel, was termed the last word in a sonnet. "Sanguillah," with its "Laureate, Laureate, chanting like a child of a gold moonland," was said to be exquisite. Still another critic said the collection "exhibits a mature poignancy that is very rare in these days of so much youthful effusion in verse. And from **New York Times: "Deep River** contains some of the finest lyrics in American poetry."

In 1969 **How Wild Was My Village** blended character and narration. Set in a small coastal town in the early twentieth century, "where nothing ever happens," Rutledge reveals the joy, hatred, anquish, and love of the people who lived there. Reminiscent of the voices in **Spoon River Anthology,** speakers from the past come back to tell the turmoil that existed beneath outward calm. According to Rutledge in his foreword, the confessions were made to help others make wiser choices.

Woods and Wild Things I Remember came out in 1970. The book compiles stories taken from the hundreds published in magazines through the years. In these sketches Rutledge draws pictures of the coastal wildwoods, reaching back to his early childhood days in McClellanville and at Hampton.

Collections of poems including **I Hear America Singing** and **Bright Angel** followed.

After the initial restoration of Hampton was completed, Alice and Archibald began to spend part of their time at 175 Alabama Street in Spartanburg, in upstate South Carolina. Alice's sisters lived there, and they gave Alice companionship while Rutledge was away conducting writers' workshops, attending to the duties of poet laureate, and making speeches at colleges nationwide.

In one of his commencement addresses he spoke of law. He called for a reverent attitude toward all law: nature, human, and divine. As always, he drew from his intimate knowledge of animal life to show how the lower animals obey the laws of courage, patience, and faithfulness. These same virtues, he pointed out, are essential for the happiness of human beings.

Much of Rutledge's time was spent in writing letters. Always a great correspondent, he kept up a continuous flow of letters and cards with his sons. Irvine, the youngest, wrote to his father three or four times a week and had done so for almost forty years. Once he said, "You have been the greatest influence on my life; what I have done well has been because of you."

Other letters from his sons evidence the deep feeling and respect they held for their father. Other than sharing his love for the hunt and outdoors, they shared their father's love for words. Occasionally they wrote poems to one another.

Through their correspondence with their father and one another, the Rutledge men coined many nicknames: Arch, Jr., was "Buckshot"; Irvine, "Gunpowder"; and Archibald, Sr., "Flintlock." Rutledge's rifle was "Annie Oakley."

Once when his father failed to be prompt in writing to Irvine, his son wrote, "It's a good thing I heard from you today. I was about to telegraph and ask if a Plateye had way laid you."

Irvine knew his father would enjoy that, for his sons had inherited their father's usage of the plantation expressions of his childhood.

When they were at Hampton, Alice and Archibald attended Saint James' Parish Church, built in 1760. Known as a Church of England or an Episcopal church, it still has the name of Thomas Lynch inscribed on the back of one of its pews.

Once a year the descendants of old plantation families gathered there to worship and to recall old friendships and family occasions.

Archibald and Alice, right, attend a picnic dinner at Saint James Parish Church, also known as the "Brick Church."

While Archibald was a student at Union College in 1900, he had been confirmed in the Episcopal Church. "I think I'm Episcopalian," he often said with a smile. "Actually, I am at home in any church. I just don't understand those people who try to tell me that I must belong to this or that church or swear by this or that creed to get to heaven. I have found heaven here in the hearts of men."

Honors poured upon him as Archibald continued to write poetry, novels, and hunting stories. As poet laureate he felt it a privilege to encourage young poets, and he did. When an English teacher at Aiken High

School asked him to pen a note that might inspire her students to write, he not only wrote a letter of encouragement but he wrote "To a Young Poet" especially for them.

O let not your bugle
Pine, falter or grieve;
Forever sing gallantly
What you believe.
The image keep vivid,
And blur not the story.
O pour in the wild love,
And pour on the glory.

If clear be your song,
If the music be true,
Some pilgrims, rejoicing,
Will listen to you.
And though the proud world
May pass you unseeing,
Yet many will love you
And bless you for being.

And every true song
is recorded in heaven.
You only return
The gift you were given.
High hold it in trust,
This chalice divine,
For only the noble
Should taste of this wine.

Tirelessly he wrote letters giving advice on poems submitted to him for criticism and doing whatever he could to assist other poets in getting their works published.

Holding true to his own writer's creed he had drawn up as a lad, he kept his writing void of cynicism and pessimism. "A writer has a job to tell about hopes and joys and the real things in life, but he must be careful never to corrupt his reader. You see," he said, "the writer has two rewards. The one is money, which is unimportant. The other is the gratitude of those for whom he writes.''

And this gratitude was always forthcoming to Rutledge. Letters came by the thousands telling him of hope and comfort his writings had afforded. ''You have helped me have a little more patience, a little more courage.''

Feeling that nearly all readers are traditionalists, Rutledge said, ''People like what they understand.'' Thus he used a formula for writing based on this simple truth: He ''found a subject worth writing about, made it simple, made it clear, made it reach the heart of the reader, and then made it beautiful.''

Although Rutledge once said that some poems came to him already created, he worked long and hard at his writing, polishing, cutting, and paring lines. He preferred to do his writing in the hours of early morning before others were up and about.

Having experienced loss and grief himself, he was able to feel compassion for others. When one of his sons was deeply hurt by a fellow associate, Archibald wrote ''A Song of Hope.''

> O gallant Heart, defeated,
> Now gazing toward the west,
> Where this day's splendor crumples,
> Disastrous and unblest -
> Look, till the deathlike darkness
> By stars be glorified,
> Until you see another dream
> Beyond the one that died.

Many persons who had been mistreated responded to the poem. One man from Texas wrote that he had been on the verge of suicide and the poem had saved him. He wrote to Archibald to ask what he might send him as a gift. Rutledge replied, ''A Texas arrowhead.'' The man sent him an entire collection of over three hundred arrowheads.

Later, after his son Mid was killed in a traffic accident and Arch, Jr., the most imaginative of his sons, had died, he was able to rise from his sorrow of darkness.

"I am absolutely unshaken in my faith that God created us, loves us, and wants us not only to be good but to be happy."

Much of Archibald's happiness evolved from his ability to find God in nature, as he expressed in the poem "Signature."

> On depth or height
> His proud armorial bearings are in sight:
> All beauty bears His signet and His crest.
> Upon the mountains and the sunrise shore
> His sign is set, and on the wildrose west.
> The evening star is His bright semaphore.
> All glories to His glories must attest,
> Acknowledging His sovereign signature.

Many of his readers thought him at his best with love lyrics as in "The Compass."

> Regard this compass:
> How veeringly the needle turns,
> Yet ever northward yearns,
> And at last will come
> Fatefully home.
> Even so my love
> Resembles
> The needle; for it turns to you
> And trembles.
> I from hill-country
> A parable bring:
> Deep in those woodlands sweet
> A hidden spring
> Gives a wild mountain stream
> Music to sing.

So you have given me
All my life long
Love from your wildwoods,
And strength to be strong.
Secret, mysterious
Source of my song.

Others found him at his best as a philosopher who could "take pure joy from music, who could understand the need of children for golden slippers and thereby know the true language of humanity."

If Rutledge had been successful in his attempts to write his autobiography, he might have given a full account of exactly how many books he published and of how many honors came to him.

It is known that he had more than twenty honorary degrees conferred on him, including Doctor of Literature from Furman University and the University of South Carolina and Union College. The University of South Carolina named him to Phi Beta Kappa.

His gold medals number more than thirty. Among his memberships are American Society of Arts and Letters, the American Poetry Society, and the Neucomen Society.

Reader's Digest gave him a Distinguished Service Award for more than a dozen years for his nature writings.

In 1956 Rutledge was cited for bringing honor to the state of South Carolina by a joint session of the state legislature. Under the leadership of Governor George Bell Timmerman, Jr., the citation called Rutledge "a lover of nature and a gifted singer of its praises who made it possible for those who do not create to appreciate beauty expressed in melodious terms."

Praises came from the Congressional Library, and in 1958 Rutledge was among five American poets asked to tape record poems for the National Archives.

In 1959 he was named elector to the "Hall of Fame of Great Americans."

Other honors included his being named "Nature Poet of America" by Poets Laureate International, and having his portrait presented to the South Carolina Legislature and hung in the State House.

On Archibald's eighty-six birthday in 1969, Senator Ernest F. Hollings of South Carolina paid tribute to him before the United States Senate.

Calling him the "poet of the South," he lauded him for revealing a philosophy of life "which men grope for in this age of plastic and steel computers."

During his long literary career Rutledge almost received the Pulitzer Prize twice: once he lost to Robert Frost; another time to Edna St. Vincent Millay. It is said that he lost the Nobel Prize to William Faulkner by one vote.

Even at the age of eighty, Archibald showed little evidence of slowing down. He killed a buck in his late seventies and still continued to hunt. A favorite pastime when he was not writing or entertaining was that of making walking sticks of dogwood and wild plum.

On April 7, 1967, a car traveling near Hampton struck him and broke his hip. Despite his determination, he was unable to walk again.

A little more than a year after the accident in May 1968, Alice died. Unable to care for himself, he went into a nursing home in Spartanburg.

With dreams of ever being able to return to Hampton growing dimmer, he and his remaining son, Irvine, had to face up to the future of Hampton.

After much deliberation and heart searching, Archibald and his son sold Hampton and three hundred surrounding acres to the state of South Carolina for historical preservation. The remaining woodlands were kept for the Rutledge family.

Archibald felt that because of its history and unique beauty, Hampton belonged in the public domain. It was decided in 1970 that the Department of Parks and Recreation would restore the mansion and make it into a State Park open to the public.

It was agreed that Will Alston, young Prince's son, would remain as grounds keeper. He and his wife Bertha had been there all of their lives and they would remain. Other Alstons would be employed "whenever feasible."

Though Archibald had the comfort of his friends and still received many letters, his heart once again yearned as it had in the days of his youth for coastal Carolina. He expressed this yearning in "The Mouth of the Santee."

> The river flows through landscape lost,
> By storied ruins of the past;
> The river finds the ancient coast,
> The rolling surge, the ocean vast;
> There where the craggy cedars mark
> Through vistas, opening on the foam,
> The floodtide flowing full and dark,
> The pacing of the ebbtide home.

Twenty-Six

Since early childhood when his father spoke of Archie's guardian angels, Archibald had been a believer.

The same week Hampton was sold, his Guardian Angel appeared. Fifteen years earlier his family had sold the summer place in McClellanville. That home, Archibald's second love, now came up for sale.

Breathing a prayer of thanksgiving, he purchased by telephone his old birthplace on Jeremy Creek. Eighty-seven years old and confined to bed, he came back to breathe the salt air and watch the sea gulls hover over shrimp boats.

With nurses moving around him, it was easy for the tall, thin-framed writer to remember the days of his youth there. The shadow of his beloved mother was here. Although in his childhood he had been aware that Hugh was closer to her than any of the other children, he felt very near to her now. He thought of how much she loved the stars, and sometimes he could almost hear her voice as she read aloud. He remembered being so fascinated by a story she had read about some pioneers. It had told of an American backwoodsman who asked an Indian how he discovered medicinal virtues of various herbs. The Indian had answered that he had learned from animals.

Archibald remembered being so impressed by the idea that Indians had watched sick and wounded animals and learned from them how to heal that he had decided he was going to be a doctor.

How often he had heard the tale of the monstrous tidal wave that had flooded the sandy streets in the village of McClellanville. He had been only three at the time, and his mother was at home with the six children. The water kept rising until it swept through the Rutledge home. Mrs. Rutledge had upturned a small table to make a raft. She put Archie and his younger sister on it and quickly collected some valuables and piled them on. Then with calm courage she hurried the four older children to safety on higher ground before running back for the floating babies.

She had displayed the same calm demeanor one night when the Colonel was away from the plantation. She awakened young Archie with a quiet yet firm voice. "Come put up the window for me," she said. "I hear robbers trying to break into the rice barn."

When Mrs. Rutledge shot both barrels in the direction of the barn, they heard muffled cries and wild running.

A short time later Archie saw his mother had settled in her chair again and taken up the book she was reading.

On still another occasion it was she who was given credit for saving Hampton from destruction by fire. As all the old plantation homes, Hampton was made of heart timber and roofed with cypress shingles. Everyone lived in fear of hearing the ringing of the great plantation fire bell which hung in a live oak before the house.

Martha, the cook, had burst from the house waving her apron and shouting to the top of her lungs, **"Fire! Fire! The great house is burning!"**

In moments hot smoke filled the air and showers of live sparks and cinders crackled.

When the rain barrels emptied quickly, Mrs. Rutledge formed a fire brigade to the river. Soon a steady line of brimming water buckets were being rushed toward the burning house.

Archibald recalled these and others memories of his childhood as he rested between visits from his many admirers and relatives.

He had chosen the quiet life, and it had given him much pleasure. From an early age the poets had been his heroes, and a longing had developed in him to be a writer.

Always he had accepted life as a privilege to be in communion with beauty and ancient order of the eternal rhythm of creation.

In the spring of 1973 Archibald's letters to Irvine spoke of a bluejay and a cardinal outside his window sill, and of some mallards and wild geese that were late in migrating. He enjoyed spring as he did when he had written "Spring in the South."

> All in this greenly shimmering spring,
> In dimly iridescent days,
> I hear the mated thrushes sing,
> And down the fragrant woodland ways
>
> Shy happy birds with plumage rare
> Flash through the glimmering solitudes,
> And like sweet censers swung in air,
> Perfume with song the dewy woods.
>
> the yellow pine that soars above
> The bullgrape-woven thicket dim,

Bears to the blue a song of love,
Bears to the earth the azure's hymn.

The columbine her ruby cup
Uplifts, brimful of honey rare;
The jasmine-fountain tosses up
Her saffron showers, stayed in air.

When, as a raindrop on a rose,
A white star in the red west gleams,
Peace wraps the world in deep repose,
In silence, sleep, and lovely dreams.

More magic's by the night conferred
While for a sinless world I long,
I hear a midnight mockingbird
Rebuilding Eden with a song.

On July 2, 1973, Archibald wrote to Irvine, "I am writing a cheerful poem on dying. It has one good line - 'when my King commands my spirit to be free.' " And as he had done for many years in letters to his sons, he signed his letter with the drawing of a flintlock.

On September 15, just five weeks before his ninetieth birthday, South Carolina's patriarch of letters and poet laureate for thirty-nine years died in the same room in which he was born in Little Hampton.

He was laid to rest in the family plot beside his son Arch, Jr. Under spreading oaks and magnolias of his beloved home by the river, the plantation Negroes sang spirituals at his graveside.

In Archibald Rutledge's poems and writings he became a minstrel singing of nature. He was a gentle singer of the South, but the songs he sang "through the throats of native birds and wildlife were the songs of America." As he expressed in his poem "The Few":

The songs that poets sing are mortal, too;
But most miraculously in a few
The granite of eternity lies hid.
The great song builds his own proud pyramid.

Bibliography

Selected works by Archibald Rutledge:

Beauty in the Heart. New York: Fleming H. Revell Company, 1903.

"Boyhood in a Rice Field," **Southern Living,** April 1969.

Children of the Swamp. New York: Doubleday and Company, 1927.

Deep River. Columbia, South Carolina: The R.L. Bryan Company, 1960.

Home by the River. New York: The Bobbs-Merrill Company, 1941.

How Wild Was My Village. Columbia, South Carolina: Wing Publications, Inc., 1969.

It Will Be Daybreak Soon. New York: Fleming H. Revell Company, 1908.

Life's Extras. New York: Fleming H. Revell Company, 1928.

Love's Meaning. New York: Fleming H. Revell Company, 1943.

My Colonel and His Lady. New York: Bobbs Merrill Company, 1956.

Santee Paradise. New York: Bobbs Merrill Company, 1956.

The Woods and Wild Things I Remember. Columbia, South Carolina: The R.L. Bryan Company, 1970.

Tom and I on the Old Plantation. New York: Frederick A. Stokes and Company, 1918.

When Boys Go Off to School. New York: Fleming H. Revell Company, 1935.

Other sources:

Archibald Hamilton Rutledge Papers (1860-1973). Prepared by Loulie Latimer Owens. University of South Carolina Manuscript Department, 1972-74.

We Called Him Flintlock. Compiled by Irvine H. Rutledge. Columbia, South Carolina: The R.L. Bryan Company, 1974.

Tapes and interviews with Kenneth Toombs, personal friend of Archibald Rutledge and Director of Libraries, University of South Carolina.

Clippings from **The State** newspaper, including Jan Wongery, September 7, 1969, and Bill McDonald, October 27, 1978.